VOID

Library of
Davidson College

Project Decision Making
in the Public Sector

Project Decision Making in the Public Sector

Alan Abouchar
University of Toronto

Lexington Books
D.C. Heath and Company/Lexington, Massachusetts/Toronto

Library of Congress Cataloging in Publication Data

Abouchar, Alan.
  Project decision making in the public sector.

  Includes bibliographies and index.
  1. Expenditures, Public—Cost effectiveness.
2. Expenditures, Public-Rate of return. I. Title.
HJ7461.A26   1984   350.72   83-49463
ISBN 0-669-08015-2 (alk. paper)

Copyright © 1985 by D.C. Heath and Company

All rights reserved. No part of this publication may be reproduced
or transmitted in any form or by any means, electronic or mechanical,
including photocopy, recording, or any information storage or retrieval
system, without permission in writing from the publisher.

Published simultaneously in Canada
Printed in the United States of America on acid-free paper
International Standard Book Number: 0-669-08015-2
Library of Congress Catalog Card Number: 83-49463

To Ann
"Let me count the ways."

Contents

List of Figures   ix

List of Tables   xi

Preface   xiii

1 The Public Sector and Cost-Benefit Analysis   1
   Applicability of Cost-Benefit Analysis   1
   Plan of Book   6
   Bibliographic Note   9
   References   10

Part I Costs, Prices, and Pricing Policy   13

2 A Classification of Costs   15

3 Pricing and Public-Sector Activities   21
   Reasons for Public-Sector Participation   21
   Economic Efficiency and Public-Sector Pricing   22
   A Possible Exception to LTFCR for Efficiency-Related
      Projects   24
   Problems   26
   Bibliographic Note   42
   References   43

4 Shadow Values   45
   Miscellaneous Discrepancies   45
   Labor and Wages   46
   Fiscal Distortions   48
   Capital   52
   Problems   54
   Bibliographic Note   59

Part II Decision Criteria 61

5 **Comparing Benefits over Time 63**

Net Present Value 64
The Internal Rate of Return 73
Financial Analysis versus Economic Analysis 75
Conclusion 77
Problems 79
Bibliographic Note 91

6 **Principles of Benefit Measurement 93**

The National Income Approach 93
The Essence of National Income Calculations 95
Problems 98
Bibliographic Note 107

7 **Infrastructure Decisions in Fully Employed Economies 109**

Benefits of a Local Infrastructure Project 109
Network Projects 115
Problems 118

8 **Project Decisions in the Underdeveloped Economy 129**

Relationships Among Benefit Measures 130
Shadow Values 131
Problems 133

9 **Consumer Surplus 139**

Historical Background 139
Inconsistencies in Application 140
Appendix 9A Marshall: Consumer Surplus, and the Marginal Utility of Money 145
Problems 147
Bibliographic Note 149

10 **Taking Account of Inflation 151**

Generalized Inflation 151
Differential Inflation 152
Problems 154

Index 159

About the Author 165

List of Figures

1–1. Venn Diagram Showing Public Sector Decisions and Cost-Benefit Analysis 2

1–2. Historical Evolution of Demand 5

3–1. Indifference Curve Analysis of Consumer's Welfare under Project Construction and Lump Sum Payment for Basic Facility 25

3P–1. Mary's Demand Curve for Caviar 27

3P–2. Individual Demand Curves for Caviar 28

3P–3. Market Demand Curve for Caviar 28

3P–4. Anoprosthetic Demand Curve for Jars of Caviar 29

3P–5. Demand for Rail Movement between A and B (Situation 1) 32

3P–6. Demand for Rail Movement between A and B (Situation 2) 35

3P–7. Demand, Average Blended Payment, and Utility Loss 36

3P–8. Demand and Surface Repair Cost (Homogenous Traffic) 37

3P–9. Police Demand: Sally, Henry, and Market 39

4–1. Basic Congestion Analysis 55

5–1. Two-Period Consumption Frontier 68

5–2. Two-Period Consumption Equilibrium 69

5–3. Incorporation of Nonmarketable Consumption, for example, Time Saving, into Consumption Frontier 70

5–4. Two-Period Consumption-National Income Frontier 72

5P–1. Two-Period Consumption Trade-off: Anticipated and Actually Experienced 81

5P–2. Comparison of NPV and IRR 87

6P–1. Traditional Consumer Surplus Diagram 98

6P–2. Two Situations with Different Tastes and Consumption Patterns and Consistent National Income Comparisons 101

6P–3. Two Situations with Different Tastes and Consumption Patterns and Conflicting National Income Comparisons 102

7–1. Typical Cost Curves for a Large Truck of Given Configuration and Load (Showing Net Social Cost at Annual Volume x') 116

7P–1. Analysis of Congestion for Bridge Situation 120

7P–2. Deadweight Loss when Discrimination Is not Possible and when Discrimination Is Possible 126

9–1. Calculation of Change in Consumer Surplus from Bridge Investment 142

List of Tables

2–1. Examples of Cost Elements Which May Partake of Different Groups of Characteristics   18

3P–1. Classification of Elasticity of Demand and Optimal Prices for Mary and John in Two Situations   31

3P–2. Calculation of Traffic Flows in Equivalent Traffic Units   38

4–1. Treatment of Duties for Shadow Adjustments   51

5P–1. Prime Rate, Inflation Rate, and Unemployment Rate   82

5P–2. Analysis of NPV under Capital Rationing   84

5P–3. Financial Analysis of Ecalpon Cement Corp

6–1. Basic Setup of National Accounts   97

7–1. Benefits and Costs of Bridge Replacement of Ferry   111

7P–1. Net Benefit Stream of Bridge Option   122

7P–2. Comparison of True Growth and "Rule of 72" Estimates   127

8P–1. Calculation of Net Annual Benefit for Two Road Designs under Two Treatments of Labor Cost   133

8P–2. Effects of Irrigation Project (First Ten Years of Operation)   135

8P–3. Calculation of Annual Benefits, Costs, and Net Benefits of Irrigation Project   136

9P–1. Consumer Surplus Calculations for Four Consumer Durables   148

Preface

The public sector has become one of the main participants in economic activity in both modern and underdeveloped economies—capitalist, socialist, and all shades in between. For this reason a theory of rational public sector project decision making has become one of the most vital areas of economic analysis. There is an urgent need for an unambiguous set of rules to aid the public sector in deciding what projects it should undertake. A trove of books has been produced to address this need, but they often conflict in their recommendations, and passions flare in the field when adherents of one view encounter advocates of another.

After teaching project evaluation for ten years at the University of Toronto, I hoped to write a book which would distill from the wide range of writings on the subject final and consistent answers to the difficult questions facing the analyst: should the internal rate of return or discounted present value be used? What should the discount rate be? How should benefits be measured? What shadow price adjustments should be made for wages, tariffs, and so on? But over the years final answers proved elusive, as solid counterarguments appeared just when one issue seemed settled. Finally, I saw that there were two obstacles to comfortable understanding and agreement: the first was that we were trying to do too much when we hoped to fit everything into a cost-benefit mold; the second was the fact that different writers have quite different implicit or explicit assumptions when developing their arguments, and the possibility had to be recognized that two apparently opposed positions were in fact reconcilable by granting that each might be appropriate in the special conditions assumed by the author.

Thus, it became obvious that a cookbook approach with its appearance of authority and certainty could be pursued only at the sacrifice of relevance. For the truth is that many projects simply do not lend themselves to comparison with others, and to suggest that some centralized investment procedure be followed for all projects imposes an impossible burden on the central planner; attention should instead be directed to trying to devise or ensure organization and procedures about whose tendency to promote efficiency one can have a reasonable degree of confidence. More attention must be paid to how projects should be financed and who should ultimately pay for them.

This is especially pressing in an era of runaway deficits when thinking about public sector expenditures risks being guided exclusively or mainly by macroeconomic concerns—inflation, employment, and interest rates—with insufficient regard for efficiency of projects and income distribution: thus, it may be all too easy, for justifiable reasons of macroeconomic policy, to clamp down on public expenditures and create inefficiency at the microeconomic level without considering the usually very plausible and efficient third option of performing the project, without affecting the public sector deficit, by revamping the user charge structure.

Moreover, many traditional concepts of project decision making cannot be decided upon on a black-or-white basis. It is not so much that the world is gray, but that sometimes black and sometimes white should be used. Are tariffs costs? It depends on their function and purpose (which are not always easy to determine). Should consumer surplus (CS) be used to measure benefits? It depends on the stability of the underlying demand curves, whether, essentially, big changes or small occur as a consequence of the investment. This means that if changes in activity levels are small, CS may be used, but it will add little to the measured benefit. Does profit maximization by public sector or state-owned enterprises (SOEs) accord with social welfare maximization, and can it provide an efficient alternative to centralized decision-making for a wide range of projects? Is self-financing of projects through municipal revenue bonds inefficient because it introduces the need for unnecessary payment collection mechanisms, as often argued, or does it provide a mechanism parallel to private sector profit maximization? Does the federal tax exemption, as practiced in the United States, distort investment allocation, obviating any advantage that might otherwise inhere in the procedure?

But the inability to prescribe absolute rules or recipes will not dishearten us if we think about all the assumptions we implicitly make when we draw the analogy with the cookbook approach in the first place. A cookbook is useful only if we have decided what we want to eat and, at the least, that we want to eat at home. But first we must decide whether home or restaurant is our preference, and even whether it is food or some other form of consumption that we want. In this book, for those projects which can be compared, we apply cost-benefit analysis and try to provide the recipes, but, since the economy embraces so many sectors and functions that cannot be compared through this analysis, we must learn how to make decisions for them which are consistent with optimization within the class of projects which can be compared.

Even without a cookbook, however, we can deepen our understanding of the procedures and the complex issues involved by the problems following each chapter (after the second). Readers are urged first to read the entire chapter (they are all rather short) with whatever degree of intensity they feel comfortable with and then attempt to work out the problems before turning to my proposed solutions.

Many problems have unambiguous solutions and may be considered as landfalls to make sure we are working against the same mechanical background understanding—calculations of traditional price theory, present values, and so on. But for others the problem is precisely to determine what is meant by words and phrases that lose much of their meaning when we try to fit our traditional theory to the real world—fixed costs, incremental costs, shadow prices, capital productivity, public goods. For these a solution different from mine may occur to a reader, but it may be no less valid for the conditions implicitly assumed.

An important part of the economist's training is the ability to determine precisely the assumptions behind any theoretic result in order that its conclusions and relevance for a particular situation under study might be objectively assessed. This is especially true in an area dealing with economic policy, since, in the real world, distinctions are much fuzzier than in a theoretic derivation. This conditionality may be disconcerting to those who approach the book hoping to find absolute answers or unqualified techniques essentially independent of the economic and social conditions of the problem. Engineers and persons trained in formal economic theory may be particularly distressed, but we should then remind ourselves that even in higher mathematics conclusions are drawn only within carefully defined assumptions; words and phrases take on entirely different meanings depending on the nature of the discussion: "space" can imply a simple collection of elements, as in a sample description space, or the domain or range of an arbitrarily specified mapping, including figures such as a torus or sphere, or it may imply a carefully defined structure of manipulation rules, as, for example, a vector space, not to speak of space itself as Euclid or the man from NASA might know it. Vector spaces may deal with arrows and real numbers, but they may also involve nth degree real polynomials, continuous real-valued functions on the closed unit interval, or real (or complex) $m \times n$ matrices as the "vectors." On the other hand, only arrows are vectors when vector fields are discussed. The careful mathematician is ever alert to the shifts in meaning that accompany his changing focus. Evidently, economics is not alone in its need to specify carefully the framework within which conclusions or rules are derived and the corresponding conditionality attached to them.

The audience for the book is expected to be diverse. It will include, in the first place, project planners from, typically, the ranks of economists, engineers, or management in private industry and the public sector. They should have enough economics background to follow discussions about capital productivity and interest, joint costs, fixed costs, real output, and depreciation as economic and accounting categories, to be aware of the limit on what formal techniques can achieve, and to be able to think rigorously about things that cannot be rigidly defined, such as shadow prices. For this group, especially, many of the problems will constitute a review or refresher of economic ideas and definitions which may have long been passive. Others who, I hope, may find the book of value are students now training in one of the above-named fields. This second group may have more time to question the solutions I propose; the first, more experience.

I hope that any reader feeling uneasy about the problems will not hesitate to write and stimulate further dialogue, for which I would be most grateful. For now, I would like to express gratitude for earlier challenges from the floor in my project evaluation class, as well as in other courses, and add the hope that the students learned as much from the experience as I did. My gratitude to Patricia Bennett, whose cheerful and skillful word processing of the many revisions and corrections made writing the book much less trying, cannot be exaggerated.

Finally, I want to thank my wife, whose zeal for me to write this book has at times exceeded my own. It is to her that the book is dedicated, with the promise that soon I will get the pictures hung.

Project Decision Making in the Public Sector

1
The Public Sector and Cost-Benefit Analysis

Since many readers may come to this field with the belief that public-sector project decision making and cost-benefit analysis are the same thing, it will be best to start by showing why they are not. Their differences and the need to consider many other factors in investment decisions are the subject of the first section. An outline of the rest of the book is given in the second.

Applicability of Cost-Benefit Analysis

Throughout the last three decades economists have tried to elaborate criteria to enable public-sector decision makers to reach the best decisions about potential investment projects. In the ultimate ideal, public-sector decision making was viewed as an integrated control system feeding upon and commensurating qualitatively dissimilar inputs and providing information on the optimal choice and sequence of investment projects. At their most ambitious, such hopes have envisaged a central decision-making apparatus to process information on the cost and benefit time streams for all possible projects and combinations of projects, with shadow prices applied as appropriate, reducing them to common terms by appropriate discount rate, and assigning tasks and budgets to executive agencies for final performance.

Since we often equate the theory of optimal public-sector project decision making with cost-benefit analysis, it will be helpful to indicate their relationship and show their differences. We may conceive of all public-sector project investment decisions as the set G_1 in the Venn diagram in Figure 1-1. Some of these can be decided through the use of cost-benefit analysis, which employs a criterion to measure all good and bad impacts on society. But others, as we will see, cannot be so decided, and it is one of our objectives to know when a partial criterion may *tend* to yield desirable results. It is sometimes impossible to compare benefits of one project with those of other projects, thus precluding use of cost-benefit analysis; then revenue bond financing, or financing out of currently generated user charge revenues, *may* promote the right decisions. On the other hand, cost-benefit analysis may

2 • Project Decision Making in the Public Sector

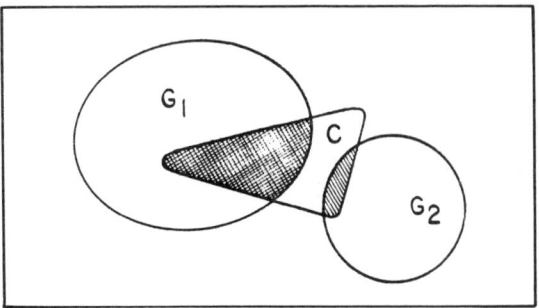

G_1 Set of Public Sector Investment Projects
C Decisions Amenable to Cost-Benefit Analysis
G_2 Set of Public Sector Non-Investment Decisions

Figure 1-1. Venn Diagram Showing Public-Sector Decisions and Cost-Benefit Analysis

also be used by a private firm attempting to optimize its decisions. For example, it may make sense to write off an asset and sell it at a loss, thus decreasing the firm's current accounting profits but improving the long-term outlook.

The set of all projects decidable by cost-benefit analysis is designated C. Then the intersection of G_1 and C contains the public-sector project investment decisions decidable by cost-benefit analysis (the cross-hatched area in figure 1-1). The relative complement of C in G_1 (the unshaded part of G_1) contains public-sector investment decisions which cannot be compared by centralizing cost-benefit analysis. For example, many highway network expansion projects, airport additions, power projects, cultural physical infrastructure (opera houses, domed stadiums), and public-sector manufacturing activities cannot be compared through cost-benefit analysis for a variety of reasons, especially when they are in different regions: existing price distortions may provide inefficient market signals, thus leading to incorrect inactivity levels in the first place; the nature of the benefits may be quite irreconcilable with others; the distribution of benefits may exacerbate income inequality; or the project may bring about radical transformation of an area or sector with insurmountable "index number" problems.

There are also public-sector decisions which can be analyzed by cost-benefit analysis but which are not investment decisions. This groups includes matters as diverse as administration of highway weight limitations and the effect of "tax expenditures," that is, exemptions from taxation of activities which would otherwise be taxed the same way as certain other comparable activities. If we regard all government economic decisions which do not deal with project investments as a set G_2, the intersection of G_2 and C contains all the noninvestment public-sector decisions to which cost-benefit analysis may be applied.

Finally, the unshaded area of C would comprise the non-public sector decisions to which we might apply cost-benefit analysis.

The hope for a single cost-benefit criterion for investment decisions has increasingly come to be recognized as too optimistic. A more satisfactory approach is to acknowledge the inherent incomparability of different classes of activity or different regions in the economy and to proceed in a more modest fashion in which local or sectoral public-sector agents make decisions which are optimal from their viewpoint, while yet not contravening the larger national goals of economic welfare.

Thus, the economics of project decision making must cast a wider net than that subsumed under the heading of "cost-benefit analysis." We believe that it is most useful to distinguish four types of procedure for reaching the best project decisions. These are characterized by:

1. efficient-budget constraints based on user charge revenues, typified by a highway network with correctly designed user charges (fuel taxes, other taxes, tolls);
2. efficient-demand projections—for example, airport traffic projections with efficient allocation of incorporation of joint costs in the price base;
3. profit maximization by state-owned enterprises (SOEs);
4. an overall or summary welfare measure based on all benefits and costs, the traditional cost-benefit analysis but applied within a much narrower range of decisions than has been believed possible.

It will be obvious as we proceed that the earlier hope of a single economy-wide optimizing criterion has not been achieved and probably never can be. The effects over time of a local tunnel are simply too different from the effects of a new airport, coal terminal, or steel plant for them to be compared in any meaningful way. Even comparison of functionally similar projects within different regions, with investment funds to be provided out of general tax revenues, is not possible, since many of the qualitatively similar benefits in the different regions have different values. For example, time savings in a high-income region are worth a great deal more to the local inhabitants than time savings in a low-income region are to its inhabitants. If general funds support the projects with the greatest returns, we tend to reinforce the existing income inequalities, since a dollar of investment will buy a greater time value benefit in the richer region. This, of course, has been recognized, but the procedure often proposed to deal with it—adjusting the time value in one of the regions—will also fail, since if we raise the time value in the poorer region, we will distort investment between this whole sector and other sectors, and if we lower the time value in the richer region, it may be forced to undertake the local investment anyway and provide income to the poorer region, in excess of that which had earlier been deemed desirable implicitly by the political process, through regular interstate transfers in the form of health or education grants or concessionary loans. (We will use "state" as the basic political unit under the central government, although in many countries provinces are the next unit in the hierarchy.)

A second point to stress is the fact that the word "efficient" is an integral part of the statement of the first two types of project decision procedures. This cannot be emphasized enough. All too often, project decisions have been based on projection of demands which may be very inefficient. This happens because we project a physical demand series forward on the basis of historical experience, possibly analyzed through a simulation model to account for the future evolution of important causal variables. But we too seldom ask whether the historical experience represents an efficient accommodation of demand. The situation is illustrated in figure 1–2, which shows for three typical years the demand curves for a service, such as airport landings, for example. At the prices provided in each year, the equilibrium output levels, given by the corresponding supply–demand intersection points A_t, are denoted q_t. In panel b these output levels are shown as points on a curve showing the historical experience. All too often this is the curve which is projected forward, and it gives the impression of the need for a large investment to accommodate the increased requirement. However, it frequently is the case that the socially efficient equilibrium is given by points which are to the left of the A_t. Consumers need not pay these higher prices because they are given either an explicit or implicit subsidy. Were consumers required to pay the full incremental costs of their actions, the points B_t would be observed. These points would then represent points on a socially *efficient* historical demand curve which is below the historically observed, socially *inefficient* demand curve, and, were it to be projected forward, there would be much less apparent need for capacity expansion.

The same warning applies to the use of budgets determined by haphazard legislative practice to delimit the set of projects to be invested in within any sector. We believe that it is part of the job of the project decision-maker to identify and call public attention to such procedures and urge that budgets be more efficiently established. This can be done by instituting correct user charges for services—electric power, highway transportation, or airport use, for example.

Thus, it should be made very clear at the outset that to say we cannot achieve a project decision-making criterion which can be applied everywhere in the economy does not mean that whatever practices are actually encountered should be accepted without question. This attitude is increasingly being recognized in public policy circles, although it is still given much less attention and emphasis than is its due.

The Public Sector and Cost-Benefit Analysis • 5

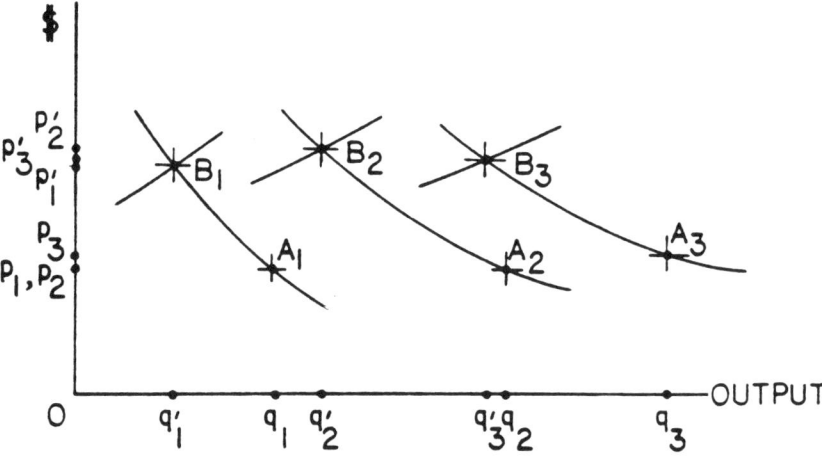

Figure 1–2a. Supply–Demand Intersections for Three Points of Time

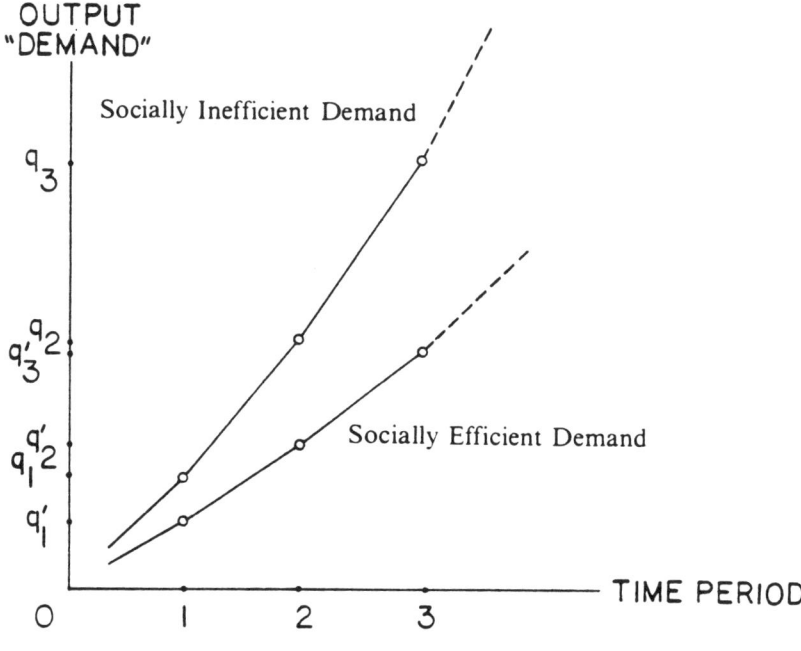

Figure 1–2b. Two "Demand" Time Series

Plan of the Book

If there were an omniscent planner who truly knew everyone's preferences and preference paths at any given time and under variations in the surrounding environment, there would be no need for a system of prices to transmit information about personal tastes and preferences. But it is precisely because no such omniscience can be assumed that the search for a single economy-wide project decision criterion is frustrated. Prices *are* necessary, and they must be rationally devised to transmit the most information while not frustrating the achievement of other aspects of socio-economic well-being. These two requirements of the price structure complicate the problem of deciding what constitutes an efficient budget constraint and determining what constitutes socially efficient demand. Accordingly, this must be the first topic of discussion.

Three aspects of the pricing structure are the subject of part I. First (chapter 2) we present certain modifications of traditional microeconomic cost analysis to allow for the much greater variety of types of costs which are relevant from the viewpoint of pricing and project decision making. This is an attempt to introduce greater flexibility into the traditional definition of costs to enable it to handle the wide variety of costs arising in practice, as well as more realistic situations in which inputs may or may not be joint depending on the demand curves.

Chapter 3 outlines the principles that must provide the framework for pricing policy for public-sector activities. Income distribution and stabilization objectives have clear implications for less-than-full-cost recovery, but activities undertaken to promote economic efficiency do not. Policy, rather, must depend on the characteristics of specific situations, and it is important to recognize and to analyze them.

Chapter 4 treats shadow prices—adjustments to the actually existing market prices for inputs and outputs. We must recognize and think in terms of efficiency vs. distribution as motives, for example, for import duties and their implications for shadow adjustments. Similar considerations affect the handling of indirect taxes. In addition, the simple but important point is made that the difference between social and private costs may frequently comprise nothing more subtle than the failure to incorporate essentially variable costs in the market price for public-sector activities, even though they are made as part of the investment expenditure. Important dimensions of output are also frequently neglected—for example, axle weight as the main determinant of highway degradation. This analysis builds on the cost classification of chapter 2.

Part II presents the decision criteria. Chapter 5 deals with the comparison of benefit and cost time streams. A discount criterion is needed to compare costs and benefits occurring at different periods of time. This discount factor must reflect both the productivity of capital and the social rate of time preference. But one does not check Friday's *Financial Post* or *Wall Street Journal* to find out what these measures were last week in the same way that one consults them to check out the central bank discount rate or the ninety-day treasury bill, and it must be determined which, if any, of the observable and usually tabulated financial rates correspond to the theoretic concepts we are seeking. The traditional analysis of this issue uses as a discount rate the absolute value of the slope of the tangent line (minus 1) at the point where the intertemporal production frontier is tangent to the (highest) social indifference curve. However, the production frontier is traditionally cast in terms of consumption in two time periods, whereas many of the investments actually undertaken are in investment goods producing sectors. Moreover, discounted present value implicitly assumes that any year's benefit may be reinvested, although, of course, benefits such as time saved on recreational, and even many work commutation, trips cannot be. These and other nettlesome issues must be reconciled before this traditional analysis can be applied, even at the conceptual level. This done, a numerical value for the discount rate can be proposed.

Of course, the proposed rate may be wrong, but the ill effect of any such misstatement is reduced by limiting its use in the first place, rejecting insistence on developing a single criterion for use throughout the economy. There are organizationally or functionally different parts of the economy for which other criteria may apply. In this case different specific tools may be used: internal rates of return for efficient-budget constraints, revenue bond financing (provided that efficient ground rules are followed for such instruments), or net profit streams for many or most SOE-type activities. The area for which the single discount criterion is needed will be seen to shrink sharply.

Also discussed in chapter 5 is the distinction between financial and economic analysis, and the need for both is explained. Economic analysis is of major interest from the viewpoint of social welfare maximization, but financial analysis is also relevant and should be applied as a check against wastefulness and excess expenditure—what we might call "plant floor inefficiency." Ways are discussed to reconcile them, including granting explicit subsidies for shadow-adjusted wages and more frequent use of discount rates comparable to the interest rates which such activities are charged in the private sector.

Concerning the measurement of benefits, three different approaches can be distinguished: rectangular measures, triangular (or trapezoidal) measures, and physical measures. Use of physical measures must presuppose that the physical quantities being demanded are efficient, as discussed above. By "rectangular measures" we mean the local or regional variants of national income measures such as GNP or GNE (Gross National Expenditure). We argue that the rectangular framework is the most consistent and efficient for analyzing both benefits and costs. Triangular measures (the several variants of consumer surplus), we believe, normally should be avoided. However, this is not the same as excluding possible benefit components which are not actually realized in purchase and sale through the market. Moreover, our rectangular approach provides clear guidance and resolution of the question of how the measures that are accepted as being appropriate conceptually should be valued, either directly or through surrogates. These are the subjects of chapter 6.

After settling on the general framework, we turn in chapter 7 to infrastructure decisions in the fully employed economy (including fully employed regions of underdeveloped countries). A number of lessons emerge. First, the difficult challenge of actually measuring and predicting changes in national income by tracing through the secondary and subsequent effects of individual investment projects often can be avoided by using surrogate measures such as cost reduction since the reduced inputs will be taken up elsewhere in the economy. Another important lesson is that the need for such projects is likely to be exaggerated when users and their benefits are not closely linked to the investment funds. Projects whose benefits are principally local in nature—and this covers many more projects than is often supposed—must be paid for locally unless there is some income distribution goal that can be *most efficiently* served by this project rather than by some other means. Local demands must be manifested by expressing this willingness through user charge contributions or an explicit political decision—for example, a referendum. Network activities must also be guided by user charges.

In chapter 8 the methodology is applied to the underdeveloped economy (including secularly unemployed regions of developed economies). Here surrogate measures, such as cost reduction or profit increases, cannot be applied, and it is necessary to investigate second-round and subsequent impacts of the investment. For this, we must use national accounts-type estimation directly. The national accounts rectangular approach also enables us to resolve many vexatious problems in the areas of labor shadow prices and distributional weights to help resolve issues of equity first raised in chapter 4.

Chapter 9 is a brief treatment of consumer surplus. This construct has been frequently misapplied in project decision making. But to understand why it leads to exaggerated benefits and distorts investments, a critical review of both its theory and application is necessary. Although Marshall's name is usually associated with it, the approbation implied thereby is unjustified. Marshall had very serious reservations about the construct and, I suspect, would have reacted with alarm to its widespread post–World War II acceptance.

In chapter 10 the implications of inflation are examined. Until the late 1970s, inflation could be safely omitted from this book: in developed economies there was little inflation to worry about; in developing economies the relative price changes were considerably less important than changes in the overall price level, so future benefits and costs, for the most part, could be expected to rise in nominal and real terms comparably in all sectors of the economy without causing distortions in intersectoral project comparison. This is scarcely the case today: relative price changes (which also lead to general price inflation) are important. Furthermore, government expenditures, including expenditures on investment projects, in turn influence inflation, and this macro feedback cannot be neglected. In addition, in our treatment (where depreciation and capital cost allowances are viewed, for the most part, as merely a convenient way of incorporating into the price base the large part of capital investment expenditure, which, in reality, comprises output-variable inputs, rather than as a calculation according to arbitrary rules), in order to efficiently price the outputs of the activity, we cannot avoid dealing with inflation. Finally, public sector or crown corporations must take account of inflation to forecast revenues to analyze and decide their own investments.

To help the flow of ideas, I thought it best to put problems and solutions after most chapters, citing them when they are first relevant. (Note that diagram numbers in the problems include the letter P.) The reader is urged to first read a chapter or section, review the problems, and try to resolve or understand each before reading my proposed solution which immediately follows.

Most problems are based on some true-life episodes that the author has experienced in various countries, although many are set in the fantasyland of Ecalpon, a country where politicians, businessmen, consumers, farmers, civil servants, bankers, academics, and all others, whether led by the invisible hand or explicit mandate, are committed to social welfare maximization.

Finally, a short bibliographic note follows most chapters. This indicates some works particularly relevant to the ideas developed in the chapter. The most important general works and collections are cited following chapter 1 with subsequent reference as necessary.

Bibliographic Note

The literature on project evaluation is large and growing. While no complete bibliography will be attempted, the citations here include many of the important general works and collections. Many of them also contain extensive bibliographies on specific issues.

The survey by Prest and Turvey, originally appearing in *The Economic Journal* and subsequently reprinted in Layard and in the American Economic Association–Royal Economic Society *Surveys of Economic Theory,* is an excellent introduction to the broad range of issues in cost-benefit analysis and to many of the merits and objections to the various approaches to each. Layard's collection also contains many of the classics concerning capital charges, as well as others exploring risk and benefit measurements. The Dorfman collection shows the wide range of investments and operating activities, whose benefits economists have tried to specify. The Munby anthology contains the seminal paper of Dupuit and examples of appraisals of three widely different kinds of transport project. The U.S. Joint Economic Committee three-volume compendium is a wealth of information on principles, methodology, and actual administrative procedures relating to U.S. federal public sector activities. The books by Maas and Eckstein constitute some of the earliest formal writings on the theory of cost-benefit analysis based on water resource management.

Mishan's book translates the theory of social welfare maximization—welfare economics—into applied economics, treating a wide range of issues likely to confront the analyst and indicating some of the necessary qualifications. The works by Pearce and Lal are useful summaries of the implications of welfare economics. Harberger's book includes many case studies from which the reader may profit. The book by Little and Mirrlees, restricted to industrial projects, is especially important as the basis for much current practice regarding the use of "real," rather than "market," prices. Gittinger's book, like Lal's under World Bank (IBRD) auspices, is a testament to the great concern of the IBRD with the development of evaluation techniques. This book is especially valuable for those concerned with agricultural investments, but it can also provide useful guidance for other areas.

Many readers especially in Third World countries, may be interested in the experience in project selection criteria of the economy with the largest public-sector participation—the Soviet Union—where investment decisions have been made for over sixty years. Evaluation of the main documentary guidelines and introduction to further readings are contained in Abouchar.

Finally, readers are strongly urged to add to their library a good general text in corporate finance dealing, among other things, with amortization calculations (principal and interest) based on different rules (for example, constant blended payment, constant principal payment), cash flow, and depreciation calculations. This is urged since the public-sector analyst must be familiar with procedures recommended for pursuit by SOEs. It is also recommended for the insight that this can contribute to analysis of capital costs for public overhead projects and revenue bond financing. Also recommended is a book of mortgage tables which typically includes interest, principal, and blended payments, present values, and principal remaining, as well as other tables.

Reference

Abouchar, Alan. "The Time Factor in Soviet Investment Methodology," *Soviet Studies,* 1985.

Dorfman, Robert, ed. *Measuring Benefits of Government Investments* (Papers Presented at a Conference of Experts, 1963). Washington, D.C.: The Brookings Institution, 1965.
Dupuit, J. "On the Measurement of the Utility of Public Works," in *Transport*, edited by Denys Munby. Middlesex, England: Penguin Books, 1968.
Eckstein, Otto. *Water Resource Development*. Cambridge: Harvard University Press, 1958.
Gittinger, J. Price. *Economic Analysis of Agricultural Projects*. 2d ed. rev. and enl. Baltimore: Johns Hopkins University Press, 1982.
Harberger, Arnold C. *Project Evaluation, Collected Papers*. Chicago: Markham Publishing Co.
Lal, Deepak. *Methods of Project Analysis: A Review*. IBRD Occasional Papers No. 16, Baltimore: Johns Hopkins University Press, 1971.
Layard, Richard, ed. *Cost-Benefit Analysis*. Middlesex, England: Penguin Books, 1972.
Little, I.M.D., and James A. Mirrlees. *Manual of Industrial Project Analysis in Developing Countries*. Paris: OECD, 1968.
Mass, A. *Design of Water Resource Systems: New Techniques for Relating Economic Objectives, Engineering Analysis, and Government Planning*. Cambridge: Harvard University Press, 1962.
Mishan, E.J. *Cost-Benefit Analysis*. New York: Praeger Publications, 1971.
Munby, Denys, ed. *Transport*. Middlesex, England: Penguin Books, 1968.
Pearce, D.W. *Cost-Benefit Analysis*. London: Macmillan, 1971.
Prest, A.R., and R. Turvey. "Cost-Benefit Analysis: A Survey." In *Cost Benefit Analysis*, edited by Richard Layard. Middlesex, England: Penguin Books, 1972.
U.S. Joint Economic Committee. *The Analysis and Evaluation of Public Expenditures: the PBB System*. 3 vols. A compendium of papers submitted to the Subcommittee on Economy in Government. Washington, D.C.: GPO, 1969.

Part I
Costs, Prices, and Pricing Policy

2
A Classification of Costs

This book is concerned with measuring the value of economic activity. Sometimes we measure the value of goods and services rendered by a project; at other times we measure the value of the inputs required to undertake and operate the project. This requires, in the first place, the adoption of a consistent framework to analyze and implement costs and prices. This is the concern of part I. In this chapter we present a classification of costs which is more expanded than that of traditional microeconomic theory and is better suited to the interpretation and treatment of costs in order to decide whether to undertake projects. Chapter 3 applies the cost framework to the problem of pricing public-sector activities. Chapter 4 deals with shadow price adjustments to market prices which may need to be made in order to calculate benefits. These adjustments are also incorporated into the project's price structure, which the project users or the project network must face.

Traditional microeconomic cost theory is not flexible enough to handle the wide variety of cost categories which must be considered for rational public-sector pricing and project decision making. The traditional theory concentrates almost exclusively on fixed cost and short-run variable costs in the basic analysis, and there are logical difficulties even in specifying fixed cost in the simplest cases. For example, since the cost curves for a year are assumed to be representative of the plant life, if fixed cost is taken to be the annual amortization charge, it must be the constant blended payment of interest and principal (provided that the amortization term is equal to the plant life). But constant blended payment implies falling interest payment and rising principal repayment. What would this imply for a firm having the identical technology but using its own funds for the initial investment? There would be no obvious justification for considering it to have annually rising yearly fixed cost, but it would be inconsistent for the two identical firms to have different cost structures.

Many will say that this problem is artificial, the result of using categories which are not "really costs" but only transfers for resources whose use was committed at the time of investment. On the other hand, many critics will also object to the use of "depreciation" on the ground that it too is a financial category. Furthermore, there is little room for distinguishing between, for example, time-incremental costs, which may or may not be related to the initial investment, and fixed annual amortization costs, which, on the one hand, may be calculated against those parts of the initial investment expenditure which truly represent sunk costs, and, on the other hand, against capital assets purchased as part of the initial investment but which wear out with use, such as rail gondolas or even the rails themselves. One result of the traditional theory is that variable inputs which are part of the investment expenditure tend to be treated like a sunk capital cost rather than as a variable cost, and subsequently they are excluded from the price base when the activity in question is in the public sector, although their amortization is included when it is a private sector activity.

It should be stressed that the tradition of treating such costs differently in the public and private sectors has developed incidentally, rather than through conscious focus, while attempting to elaborate a consistent and meaningful theory of cost in the private sector. The annual fixed cost of the firm, including amortization of the investment expenditure and interest, is recovered only as a by-product of equilibrium and optimization of the firm. Price–short-run marginal cost equalization leads to a price–output configuration such that total cost per period is recovered as long as the long-run average cost curve is horizontal or U-shaped, with production taking place at the lowest point. In fact, it is very difficult to verify whether a firm's cost curve has these characteristics, and indeed, with so many dimensions of output (different commodities produced by the multiproduct firm; the time profile of output; the dimensions and characteristics of even "homogeneous" commodities such as living room chairs, as well as the fact that the demands for the different commodities are not independent) it is difficult even to define marginal cost or a marginal cost function. But since the private firm must cover its costs to remain active, the earning of a profit which is "reasonable" (in an accounting sense) is deemed as evidence of efficiency. But similar treatment—amortization and recovery of the initial expenditure—is not usually thought appropriate for public-sector activities. At best, the zero profit performance of a bridge or tunnel, as determined through repayment of revenue bonds issued to finance the facility in the first place, is accepted apologetically as a departure from optimality caused by exigencies of real world public finance and capital markets.

To think more cogently about investment and pricing policy and the very important links between them requires that we recognize a much greater diversity of costs than the traditional textbook explores. At least eight cost categories are of interest, and most individual cost elements encountered in practice partake of characteristics of more than one of these categories. What are traditionally called sunk costs, we prefer to call "isochronic costs" to convey their essence, which is that they are constant with respect to the rate of output per unit time and with respect to the passage of time. They are a component of the investment expense, a second class of cost. But apart from this, no other class is a subset of any other, so individual inputs share characteristics with costs in different classes.

The cost categories we wish to distinguish are shown in table 2–1, together with examples. The cost categories are shown in the row and column headings. Naturally, any cost in a class would fall into the diagonal intersection for that class, so to simplify presentation the diagonals are marked only with a cross. But beyond that it is interesting to see how varied the characteristics of a cost category can be. Road surface is an investment expense, a time-variable cost, and an output rate-variable cost, although the time-variability is much less than the output rate-variability. (In fact, time deterioration is much less than axle-weight deterioration, which is the most important dimension or cause of highway degradation.) Railroad administration is a recurring fixed cost (it is also a labor cost, but for our purposes we do not distinguish labor as a separate category), but interest paid on all the initial investment is also a periodically recurring fixed cost. Time-variable costs usually involve doing something, and they may be either continuous—as the year-round painting of a large bridge—or discrete, and not part of the investment, as would payment of interest or administration. However, they need not involve a new human action, the rusting of rail spikes, for example. Output-variable cost elements may include lumber for house construction, steel for nail production, or labor for dress manufacture—all of which represent typical textbook examples of variable cost—or consumption of hopper cars or steel rails as coal is shipped, inputs purchased as part of the initial investment but which wear out with use and are not typical textbook examples. Note that some examples, such as railroad administration or bridge painting, may be considered as continuously or discretely time variable, depending on whether we wish to think of the money payment for the services or the consumption of the inputs in physical terms.

One of the analytically most difficult cost categories is joint cost. Often this is taken to be isochronic cost, which it may be—for example, an excavation for a dam undertaken for a repeated annual flow of several different kinds of output (power, flood control, and so on). But it may also be an output-variable or time-variable cost, continuous or discrete. We cannot provide a single rule for pricing joint costs because of their great diversity, but we argue in chapter 3 that many inefficiencies and problems in public finance are associated with joint costs, which are often prejudicially referred to as "public goods."

It is extremely important that we recognize this diversity of costs. The main import of the classification is that many more costs than are usually

Table 2-1
Examples of Cost Elements Which May Partake of Different Groups of Characteristics

	Investment Expense	Isochronic Cost Element	Output-Variable Cost Element	Time-Variable Cost Element
Investment Expense	×	Highway grading Dam construction Mine shaft	Steel rails Road surface Coal hoppers	Steel rails Road surface
Isochronic Cost Element		×	Incompatible	Incompatible
Output-Variable Cost Element			×	Steel rails Road surface
Time-Variable Cost Element				×
Continuously Variable Cost Element				
Discretely Variable Cost Element				
Periodically Recurring Cost Element				
Joint Cost Element				

thought to vary with rate output actually do so vary. Furthermore, it is often necessary to investigate and determine the dimension of output with respect to which they vary, since this may be crucial from the viewpoint of pricing. Perhaps the best example here is highway pavement which deteriorates principally with axle weight. This was clearly demonstrated by the American Association of State Highway Officials' (AASHO) empirical tests in the late 1950s. The essential result of these tests was the fourth-power law—approximately, the ratio of damage coefficients for any two axle weights is equal to the fourth power of the ratio of these weights. If these costs are not taken into account in the pricing of the highway network (and they have not been in most countries) the result is artificial stimulation of demand—generation of what we have called socially inefficient demand—and creation of an

Continuously Variable Cost Element	Discretely Variable Cost Element	Periodically Recurring Cost Element	Joint Cost Element
Steel rails Road surface Coal hoppers	Incompatible	Coal hoppers (recurring purchase)	Railway locomotives Tunnel blasting for railway
Incompatible	Incompatible	Incompatible	Tunnel blasting
Steel rails Road surface Limestone for cement production	Bricklayer hired for house construction		Cost of railroad shuttle between points A and B, depending on directional demands (problems 3.11–14)
Fuel to heat seaway locks for winter operation Year round bridge painting	Railroad administration	Tending of highway slopes Interest on loan Opportunity cost of agricultural land used for airport	Tending of highway slopes
✗	Incompatible	Incompatible	Fuel to heat seaway locks in winter
	✗	Periodic dredging of channel	Snow removal from mountain pass
		✗	Snow removal from mountain pass
			✗

apparently socially justified need for additional highway network links or upgrading of specifications: deeper subbase, parallel links, additional lanes, and so on—as illustrated in figure 1–2.

Furthermore, very often the isochronic costs should also be included in the pricing base. This is true whenever the isochronic costs are undertaken for an expanding network—the grading of a connecting link, the extension of a subway, or the addition of a bridge to a system of river connections in a city. In all such situations we should think of the incremental costs of providing the next increment to the network as being the marginal cost to which the incremental social benefit is equalized, and if the beneficiaries do not pay for it there is a danger that, without a budget constraint, their perception of potential benefits will be exaggerated.

Finally, the distinction is sometimes made between escapable and inescapable costs, only the former being correctly included in pricing of incremental output. Often, however, what we believed inescapable turns out, on close inspection, to be escapable and, hence, properly included in the price base.

Most, or all, of the categories listed in table 2–1 are easily recognized, although they do not reconcile directly with the standard microeconomic cost categories—short- and long-run total, average, and marginal costs—or with the optimization rules based on them, except for the general dictum that incremental social cost should equal incremental utility, the latter best measured by price. But, clearly, with such a broad range of cost categories there is no simple way to define incremental cost once and for all. Moreover, the dividing lines among our categories are not as clear as we would wish. It is easy to think of at least three kinds of ambiguity:

1. some cost elements deteriorate partly with time and partly with output;

2. classification of a cost element may depend on whether the price paid for an input (the weekly wage or the payment for fuel or the consumption of the resource (the labor hour or the gallon used)) is the way we think of the input;

3. some inputs may vary continuously with time within a subperiod of the period used for the analysis, but they are discrete cost elements from the viewpoint of the latter.

3
Pricing and Public-Sector Activities

In this chapter we seek normative criteria for deciding when the public sector should involve itself in the economy and what pricing policies it should pursue. The need for appropriate pricing policies resides in the need for correct budget constraints for investment decisions, as well as for correct signals in the form of efficient physical activity projections.

Section 1, Reasons for Public-Sector Participation, summarizes the possible justifications for public-sector activity. Section 2, Economic Efficiency and Public-Sector Pricing, presents a legal–administrative approach to the definition of economic efficiency as a motive for public involvement and the pricing policies implied thereby. Section 3, A Possible Exception to LTFCR for Efficiency-Related Projects, discusses a possible exception to local full-cost recovery for efficiency-related projects which may be appropriate in certain circumstances.

Reasons for Public-Sector Participation

There are four justifications for direct public-sector participation through investment and operating expenditures. These include national–political, stabilization, income distribution, and economic efficiency objectives. This classification adds one to the usual three-way classification of public finance, first explicitly stated by Musgrave. But our finer breakdown enables us to think more clearly about pricing policies since it removes, for example, national defense or sovereignty over-flights over remote territory from the economic rubric, and enables us to state, frankly, that such decisions are a matter of noneconomic policy which economists have no special competence to judge, except insofar as they may be called upon to analyze cost effectiveness of different approaches to the national–political goals (Problem 3.1). This helps us to avoid constructs, such as "public good," which becloud discussion of price policy and normative criteria for public investment. This goal is further promoted by asking what is meant by "efficiency" in the first place.

Economic Efficiency and Public-Sector Pricing

Although stabilization and income distribution objectives have clear-cut implications for pricing policy—price so as to recover less-than-full cost from users and direct beneficiaries—projects undertaken for efficiency reasons do not. Less-than- or full-cost recovery may be appropriate, the latter being desirable except when its pursuit may introduce inefficiencies which more than offset the gains. In consonance with the basic stricture of economic efficiency, the incremental social cost should equal incremental value as measured by price; that is, the full cost, which is the incremental cost to society, must be covered by the sum of the prices people are willing to pay for all services of the activity, *unless* imposing such charges is itself costly due to the need for additional resources to levy the charge or determine people's wants—an exception which we believe to be much more limited than many people think. Although we believe this conclusion is consistent with the basic essence of marginalist theory, it may appear to conflict with some common beliefs about public-sector provision of efficiency-related activities through central general tax revenues. The arguments are well known and usually involve concepts or variations on the themes of "public goods," high collection costs, decreasing costs (with the implicit and unrealistic assumption of inability to discriminate), and inability to determine people's true demands. How may these traditional objections be answered?

1. "Public goods" are as often as not provided in the private sector. Their peculiar characteristic of having vertically additive demand curves is neutrally and, hence, more adequately conveyed by the expression "anoprosthetic demand" (Problems 3.2–3.6). If we know enough to determine the benefit from such activities, we must know enough to price them effectively; if we do not know these demands, a case cannot be made for provision by any sector in the first place. If we know the subdemands we can segregate markets and price discriminatorily to recover those cost components that are truly joint and invariable with respect to output and time—isochronic in the language of chapter 2—or output-variable and joint (Problems 3.7–3.15). Note that this approach will force us (more insistently than is usually done) to distinguish those cost elements that may in fact depend on some measure of utilization (Problem 3.16). The damage or cost variation with axle weight for the highway sector is a good example (Problem 3.17).

2. The argument (which has been used to justify LTFCR) that it simply costs too much to impose the charge and collect the revenue, even if we know the demand curves, can also be exaggerated. Current experience in imposing taxes which vary with the important use dimensions is also positive and holds great promise for the future; the so-called third-structure road taxes in parts of the United States are an excellent illustration.

3. The argument that decreasing cost activities should be paid for publicly, with only the incremental cost recovered from users, has also been overstated. Suppose there is a periodically recurring—or even continuously time-variable—cost. Clearly, the average cost of this element will decrease with the rate of output. But output is rarely so homogeneous that it is not possible to discriminate, and, indeed, any tollbooth collection schedule usually involves an attempt to discriminate. Note, furthermore, that the recovery of fixed amortization charges is accepted as a matter of fact in the private sector and rarely taken exception to.

4. Many public services commonly thought not to be susceptible to benefit-taxation principles, because recipients attempt to conceal their true demands, can indeed be paid for in this way while maintaining welfare efficiency. For example, the greater the value of the house, the greater, on the whole, is the demand for police protection, and the people do in fact pay more for this protection through property taxes (Problems 3.18 and 3.19). Public-sector provision of police services, therefore, cannot be justified on the ground of "nonexcludability" or "free riders" (Problem 3.20).

Essentially, then, for a project undertaken by the public sector for efficiency motives, full-cost recovery from users and direct beneficiaries should be pursued, except when it is reasonably clear that doing so would impose inefficiencies on the economy (Problem 3.21) by imposing high collection costs or by denying access to noncongesting users, as in the case of a bridge with little anticipated relocation effect. But the traditional assumption that the facility should be provided at no charge may stimulate socially inefficient demand, as shown earlier in figure 1–2.

Finally, in most economies the public sector includes numerous corporate entities whose presence is not easily explained by any of the four motives stated earlier. In many instances they are a historical legacy from times when their public-sector affiliation could be explained by one of these motives: for example, some national railroad lines or airways, postal services, or other such organizations, a large part of whose activity was once the political–national goal of tying together outlying areas. Sometimes they can be explained by efficiency aims, especially when the capital requirement exceeds the reasonable possibilities of the private sector, as is often the case in underdeveloped economies. A third possibility is publicly owned firms in socialist countries in which efficient resource allocation subject to the constraint of socialism is also to be sought. All of these are examples of state-owned enterprises, for which there should be no presumption of LTFCR. To the extent that they continue to serve some necessary political–national or income distribution function, some special consideration should be given, but it is much more efficient to do this through an explicit subsidy tied to the specific service than through a general LTFCR policy. It goes without saying, how-

24 • Project Decision Making in the Public Sector

ever, that just as the SOE should not subsidize users generally, neither should it be given favorable treatment in the market with respect to foreign exchange allocations, tariff preferences, exclusive routes, monopoly, and so on.

A Possible Exception to LTFCR for Efficiency-Related Projects

There is one exceptional set of circumstances which may justify participation by higher-level governments and LTFCR in projects for local jurisdictions undertaken for efficiency purposes. This requires that the welfare of people initially outside the local jurisdiction undergo a net improvement in relation to their position before the project *and* before the higher-level jurisdiction-wide tax is imposed. It is not enough that they move to the jurisdiction—"vote with their feet"—after the project is completed and the tax is imposed. The possibilities are illustrated in figure 3–1.

Imagine that urban amenities can be provided by a city as a single composite good called urbams (shown on the horizontal axis). The individual may consume any number of these and still have an income y remaining to devote to other consumption. This is given by $y = y_0 - px$, where p is the price of one urbam and y_0 is the individual's initial after-tax income. The indifference map for a consumer living outside the city today is shown in panel a. Since the price of an urbam is so high, he consumes very few at the start. His budget-line indifference curve tangency takes place at point A on I_0. To do this he must travel to the city once a week, say.

A project is built with the potential to reduce the price of consuming one urbam to p'. This gives the consumer a new budget line, which is tangent, at B, to a higher indifference curve, I_1, thus, raises his welfare. This requires him to move to the city. But the investment expenditure for the project is to be paid for by an annual tax T on everyone in the higher-level jurisdiction. This tax reduces the consumer's after-tax income from y_0 to $y'_0 = y_0 - T$. At the new price the division of his income into consumption of urbams and other goods is represented by the coordinates of point C on I_2, but he will be worse off than before. To consume so many urbams requires him to move to the city, and this is what we see that he does. However, it is clear that if he did not do this—did not "vote with his feet" and move to the city, but continued to consume as few urbams as at the start—he would be inefficiently allocating his income, since consumption would take place at point D on an indifference curve, I_3, lower than I_2.

Thus, moving, in itself, tells us nothing. For his welfare to rise over his initial position, the consumer, after moving to the city, must earn an *after-tax* income, that would permit him to attain an indifference curve higher than his initial curve I_0. This situation is shown in panel b, where after-tax income y'_0

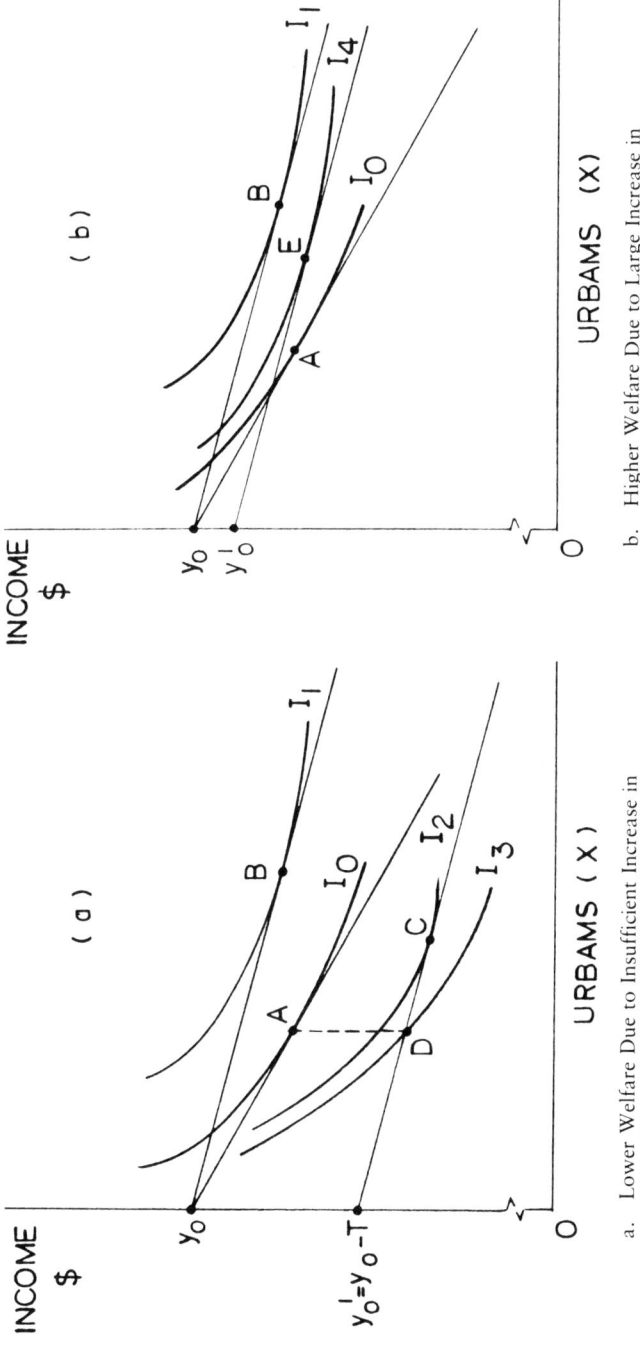

Figure 3–1. Indifference Curve Analysis of Consumer's Welfare under Project Construction and Lump Sum Payment for Basic Facility

a. Lower Welfare Due to Insufficient Increase in Gross Income

b. Higher Welfare Due to Large Increase in Gross Income

26 • *Project Decision Making in the Public Sector*

has substantially increased and nearly equals his original income, thus enabling him to reach a higher indifference curve. Unless this is known to be the result of the investment, recovery of the investment expenditure through a tax imposed at the higher jurisdiction cannot be justified. This more demanding test is not always insisted on by policymakers.

Two warnings must be given:

1. It may still be the case that payment out of general revenues of the higher jurisdiction is justified if the overwhelming majority of people there live in the local jurisdiction *and* it is very costly to collect from each consumer each time he consumes a unit.
2. We are speaking only about efficiency-related projects. If the project is income-distribution related in the first place, the higher level jurisdiction should contribute to the investment.

Problems

3.1. Some activities are traditionally or increasingly viewed as appropriate for the public sector to discharge, although it is often hard to justify this view on economic grounds of any type (distribution, stabilization, or efficiency). Ecalpon has decided to establish a national public-sector oil company called Petropon. Some view this as a national–political decision, some as a decision purely designed to satisfy patronage needs of a party in power. However, there may be a sound economic justification. Can you think of one?

Solution

The objective may be to ensure supply in case of international tension. Thus, if an international cartel threatens to embargo supplies to international oil companies as a response to political actions of their major owner nation, Ecalpon may be able to disassociate itself from the other nation's policies and ensure supplies through Petropon, but there is no reason for Petropon to operate on a less-than-full-cost recovery (LTFCR) basis.

3.2. Mary's caviar demand curve is $q(p) = a - bp$, where p is the price in dollars of one ounce of caviar, q is the number of ounces consumed per week, and $b > 0$. For $a = 40$ and $b = 8/3$, draw this curve in the standard way.

Solution

$$q = 40 - 8/3\, p, \quad p = 15 - .375q, \quad q(0) = 40, \quad p(0) = 15.$$

Pricing and Public-Sector Activities • 27

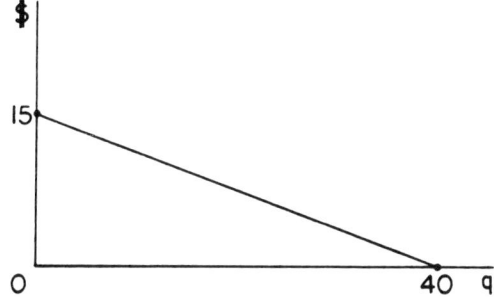

Figure 3P-1. Mary's Demand Curve for Caviar

3.3. The price elasticity of demand is defined as the relative consumption change when there is a relative price change of 1 percent: $E_p = (\Delta q/q) \div (\Delta p/p)$, where $\Delta p/p = .01$. Since this is ordinarily negative, which slows up discussion, we usually take E_p to be the absolute value of this ratio. Note that it may also be written

$$\left| \frac{\Delta q}{\Delta p} \cdot \frac{p}{q} \right|.$$

For an infinitesimal price change this becomes

$$\left| \frac{dq}{dp} \cdot \frac{p}{q} \right|.$$

For Mary, determine $E_{p|p=10}$ and $E_{p|q=20}$.

Solution

$q(10) = 13\frac{1}{3}$, $dq/dp = -2.67$, hence
$E_{p|p=10} = |-2.67 \times 10/13\frac{1}{3}| = 2.0$.
$p(20) = 7.5$, hence $E_{p|q=20} = 1.0$.

3.4. John's caviar demand curve is given by $q(p) = 25 - 1.25p$. Graph it on the same diagram as Mary's and find his elasticities at the same points.

Solution

$q = 25 - 1.25p$, $p = 20 - .8q$, $q(0) = 25$, $p(0) = 20$
$q(10) = 12.5$, hence $E_{p|p=10} = |-1.25 \times 10/12.5| = 1$.
$p(20) = 4$, hence $E_{p|q=20} = |-1.25 \times 4/20| = .25$.

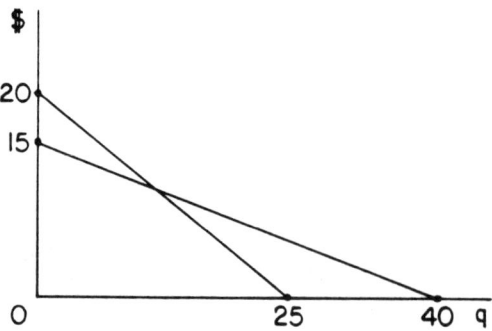

Figure 3P-2. Individual Demand Curves for Caviar

3.5. John and Mary comprise the total market. Construct the market demand equation and graph the market demand curve. Find the market price elasticity at $p = 10$.

Solution

The market demand equation is

$$q(p) = \begin{cases} 25 - 1.25p, & 0 \le q \le 6.25 \\ & (\text{or } 15 \le p < 20); \\ 65 - (1.25 + 2.67)p & 6.25 < q < 65 \\ = 65 - 3.92p, & (\text{or } 0 < p < 15). \end{cases}$$

For $0 \le q \le 6.25$, market demand coincides with John's.

For $E_{p|p=10}$ we have $q(10) = 25.8$ and

$$E_{p|p=10} = |-3.92 \times 10/25.8| = 1.52.$$

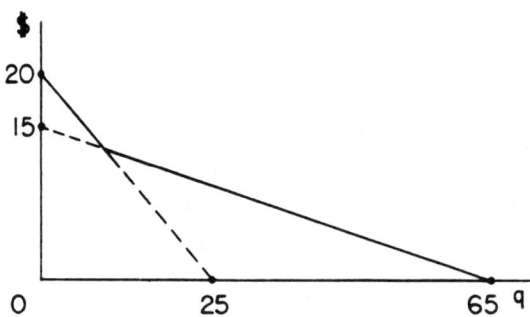

Figure 3P-3. Market Demand Curve for Caviar

3.6. Suppose now that these demand curves should be added vertically. For example, John is completely turned off by caviar, but he etches the containers in his crafts business and sells them for a good price. The caviar is imported, and John does not know the original source of the jars so for the time being he is willing to contribute part of the purchase price toward the acquisition of each jar. That is, he wants to buy jars of caviar for the sake of the jars alone, and he is willing to throw away the caviar; but if Mary wants the caviar, the price they are willing to pay together exceeds the price John is willing to pay on his own. (John's caviar demand curve would then be cast in terms of jars of caviar rather than ounces, but to keep things simple we will continue to work in ounces.) The demand for caviar is then anoprosthetic. Determine the demand function and draw it. (You will probably find it easier to work with the inverse demand function $p(q)$.

Solution

The inverse demand function is

$$p(q) = \begin{cases} (15 - .375)q + (20 - .8q) & 0 \leq q \leq 25 \\ = 35 - 1.175q, & (\text{or } 5.625 \leq p \leq 35); \\ 15 - .375q, & 25 < q \leq 40 \\ & (\text{or } 0 < p < 5.625). \end{cases}$$

This segment coincides with Mary's demand curve.

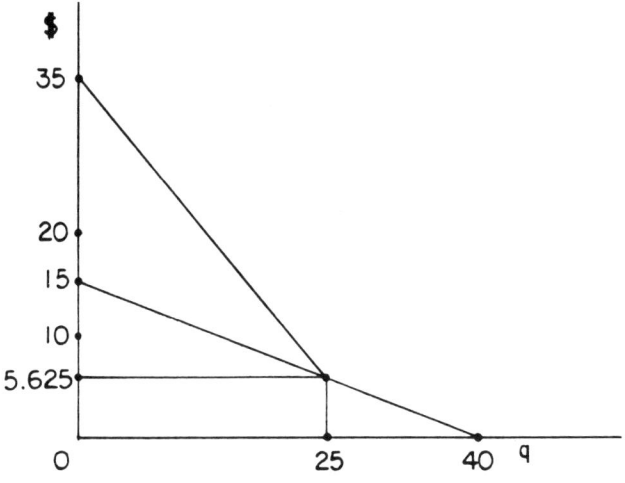

Figure 3P-4. Anoprosthetic Demand Curve for Jars of Caviar

3.7. If $11.50 is the incremental social cost, the efficient level of demand is given by $q\,(\$11.50)$. Determine $q\,(11.50)$. How should the price of $11.50 for each jar be shared between Mary and John? (Remember the basic economic optimization condition that marginal utility, represented by demand price, must equal marginal cost to each consumer).

Solution

Since $11.50 > 5.625$, we look at the part of the demand curve on which both demands are positive. We have

$$p = 11.5 = 35 - 1.175q \quad \text{or} \quad q = 23.5/1.175 = 20.$$

Then

$$p_M(20.0) = 15 - .375 \times 20 = 7.5,$$
$$p_J(20.0) = 20 - .8 \times 20 = 4.0,$$

and

$$p_M + p_J = \$7.5 + \$4.0 = \$11.5,$$

so the total cost is recovered.

3.8. Find the market price elasticity and the individual elasticities for Mary and John at the price of $11.50 for the anoprosthetic situation of problem 3.6.

Solution

Market:

$$E_{p|p=10} = |-3.92 \times 11.5/20| = 2.25,$$
$$E_{M,p} = |-2.67 \times 7.5/20| = 1.0,$$
$$E_{J,p} = |-1.25 \times 4/20| = .25.$$

3.9. Determine the market price and individual prices at a quantity of five jars per week for the situation of problem 3.6. Also calculate the price elasticities for Mary and John.

Solution

$$p(5) = 35 - 1.175 \times 5 = 29.125,$$
$$p_M(5) = 15 - .375 \times 5 = 13.125,$$

$$p_J(5) = 20 - .8 \times 5 = 16.0,$$
$$E_{M,p|q=5} = |-2.67 \times 13.125/5| = 7.0,$$
$$E_{J,p|q=5} = |-1.25 \times 16/5| = 4.0.$$

3.10. The "inverse elasticity" pricing rule says that a joint cost should be apportioned among users in inverse relation to their demand elasticities. Tabulate the results of the last two illustrations. (Insert the name of the person corresponding to each pair of characteristics (price and elasticity) in the corresponding cell.)

Table 3P–1
Classification of Elasticity of Demand and Optimal Prices for Mary and John in Two Situations

	For 3.8 ($q = 20$)			For 3.9 ($q = 5$)	
Price	Elasticity		Price	Elasticity	
	Lower	Higher		Lower	Higher
Lower	John		Lower		Mary
Higher		Mary	Higher	John	

What conclusion would you draw from this comparison?

Solution

In problems 3.8 and 3.9 we derived the optimal entrant levels and price apportionment, with each person consuming to the point where his marginal utility (price) was just equal to the price he was asked to pay. But these results conflict with the inverse elasticity rule. Therefore the inverse elasticity rule cannot be applied. We must use instead a general rule that refers to the *intensity* of demand only.

3.11. The great difficulty in generalizing specific pricing rules is illustrated by the following example. A railroad can move an empty flat car between points A and B and return for $4.00. To move a 40-ton load, with an empty return, costs $5.50; it costs $7.00 if loaded both ways. Suppose for A-bound traffic $q_A = 1200 - 25p$ and $P_A = 48 - .04q$; for B-bound, $q_B = 1170 - 30p$ and $P_B = 39 - q/30$. We must determine the quantities to be shipped and the optimal prices. Draw the demand curves. After you draw them and note that D_A lies above D_B throughout the positive quadrant, you may be tempted to suggest that the A-bound traffic be charged $(4 + 1.50) per car and the B-bound traffic be priced as a follow-on at $1.50 per carload on the ground that $1.50 represents the marginal cost. Try this approach and show that the resulting demands are incompatible with efficiency.

Solution

$$p = \begin{cases} (48 - .04q) + (39 - q/30) \\ \quad = 87 - .0733q, & 0 < q < 1170, \\ 48 - .04q, & 1170 < q < 1200, \end{cases}$$

$$q_A(5.5) = 1200 - 5.5 \times 25 = 1062.5,$$

$$q_B(1.5) = 1170 - 1.5 \times 30 = 1125 > 1062.5.$$

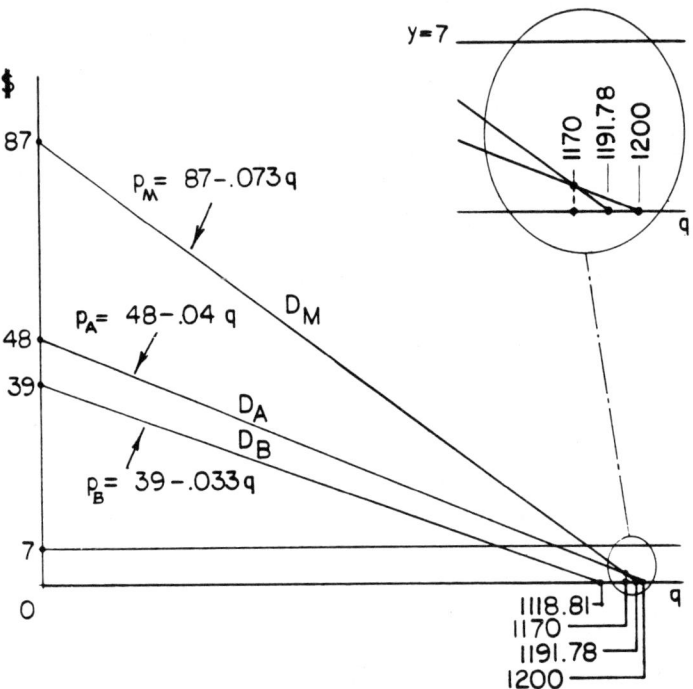

Figure 3P-5. Demand for Rail Movement between A and B (Situation 1)

Thus, at these prices more B-bound cars would be demanded than are traveling, so additional shuttles must be added. But the cost for these would be $(4 + 1.50) = \$5.50$, while B-bound pays only $1.50! Therefore, it would be inefficient to provide extra cars for the latter.

3.12. (continued). The next possibility is to consider the demand for round trips as anoprosthetic. Pursue this inquiry and determine the prices to be charged.

Solution

The round-trip, loaded shuttle price is $7.00. Inserting this into the market anoprosthetic demand equation gives $7 = 87 - .07333q$, whence $q = 1091$ (rounding). The respective directional prices are then

$$p_A = 48 - .04 \times 1091 = 4.36 \quad \text{and} \quad p_B = 39 - 1091/30 = 2.63$$

so that

$$p_A + p_B = 4.4 + 2.6 = 7.0 = p.$$

Note that each price exceeds the minimally conceivable incremental cost of $1.50.

3.13. (continued). Now suppose that the cost structure is $1.00 for the empty round-trip and $3.00 for the load in each direction. Does this affect your conclusions in 3.12?

Solution

Yes. In 3.12 the incremental cost could not be conceived to be below $1.50. Since the cost curve cut the anoprosthetic demand curve where it did, however, the whole shuttle cost was incremental and joint for the two directions. Now, however, the minimally conceivable incremental cost is $3.00, which exceeds the price of $2.63 for B-bound traffic. A-bound traffic will have to pay $1.00 + $3.00 = $4.00 per car, that is, it must pay the empty shuttle, while B-bound comes on as a follow-on incremental freight. The volumes will be:

A-bound: $p_A = 4 = 48 - .04q$, whence $q_A = 1100$.
B-bound: $p_B = 3 = 39 - q/30$, whence $q_B = 1080$.

Twenty cars will move empty in direction B.

3.14. We concluded in 3.13 that the approach of 3.12 would be wrong for the new conditions since incremental social cost exceeded incremental social utility, as measured by the price per unit of B-bound traffic demand. Calculate the individual price elasticities at the points of consumption and integrate the result into your remarks in 3.10.

Solution

The question illustrates the ambiguity of language. Does a comparison of elasticities imply comparison at the levels that will be observed (if pricing is efficient), or does it imply comparison at a given quantity. In the context of 3.12 these are the same, since both demands are realized at the same output level (1091). In 3.13 they are different.

The elasticities in 3.12 at optimal price–quantity pairs are

$$E_{A,p} = |-25 \times 4.36/1091| = .100,$$
$$E_{B,p} = |-30 \times 2.63/1091| = .072.$$

The elasticities are both low but A-bound is 39 percent higher. However, A-bound traffic pays 66 percent more!

The elasticities in 3.13 are also low and closer. (A-bound is 10 percent higher.)

$$E_{A,p} = |-25 \times 4/1100| = .091,$$
$$E_{B,p} = |-30 \times 3/1080| = .083.$$

Now A-bound traffic pays 33 percent more.

Note that in both cases a higher part of the joint cost is charged to the more elastic demand in contrast to expectations.

3.15. Finally, suppose the earlier prices ($4.00, $1.50, $1.50) continue to hold but that the B-bound traffic demand is given by $q_B = 900 - 30p$. What prices should be charged?

Solution

$$q_A = 1200 - 25p, \qquad p = 48 - .04q,$$
$$q_B = 900 - 30p, \qquad p = 30 - .033q,$$
$$p = \begin{cases} 78 - .073q, & 0 \leq q \leq 900, \\ 48 - .04q, & 900 < q \leq 1200. \end{cases}$$

At $p = 7$, we have $7 = 78 - .073q$; $q = 968$. But since B-bound traffic becomes zero at 900 and cannot contribute anything to the shuttle thereafter, this clearly will not do. So the demands must be resolved into components, again with B-bound demand as a follow-on, but at a much lower level. Solving, we find

$$p_A = 5.50 = 48 - .04q_A; \qquad q_A = 1062,$$

and

$$p_B = 1.50 = 30 - q/30; \quad q_A = 855,$$

and there are 206 empties. At the prices charged the elasticities are

$$E_{A,p} = |-25 \times 5.5/1062| = .13,$$
$$E_{B,p} = |-30 \times 1.5/855| = .05.$$

While both elasticities are low, $E_{A,p}$ is more than two and one-half times as high as $E_{B,p}$, but it pays much more (almost four times as much) for what is technologically the same service—transport between two points, A and B. Therefore, be careful in formulating pricing rules in terms of elasticities when dealing with anoprosthetic demand!

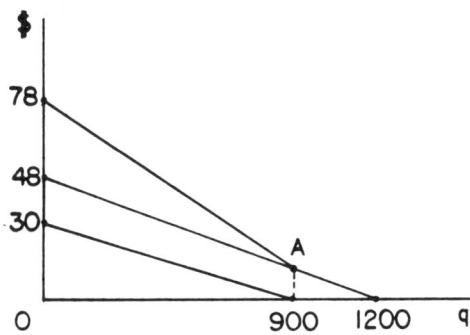

Figure 3P–6. Demand for Rail Movement between A and B (**Situation 2**)

3.16. The prototype "public good" is a bridge. Suppose its cost structure is as follows (10^6):

Construction		8.0
Annual maintenance		3.7
Painting	1.5	
Toll operation	1.0	
Road surface repair	1.2	
Total		11.7

Assume that virtually all traffic is local.

1. Draw the cost curves (keep in mind that surface damage depends on traffic volume and composition, the fourth-power law: relative damage of two vehicles is approximately equal to the fourth power of the axle-weight ratio).

2. What tolls would you charge? (Be precise in stating your assumptions.)

Solution

Several possible situations may obtain. First, suppose the bridge is expected to last fifty years and is paid for by a general purpose bond issued by the city with constant blended payment amortization over fifty years at 10 percent. Then the annual payment is $b = P \times (i/(1 - (1 + i)^{-T})) = \$806{,}873$; where P is the amount of the loan. If this is considered an annual fixed cost, if vehicles are homogeneous with demand as shown, and if the other expenditure items are neglected for the moment, the picture is shown in figure 3P–7.

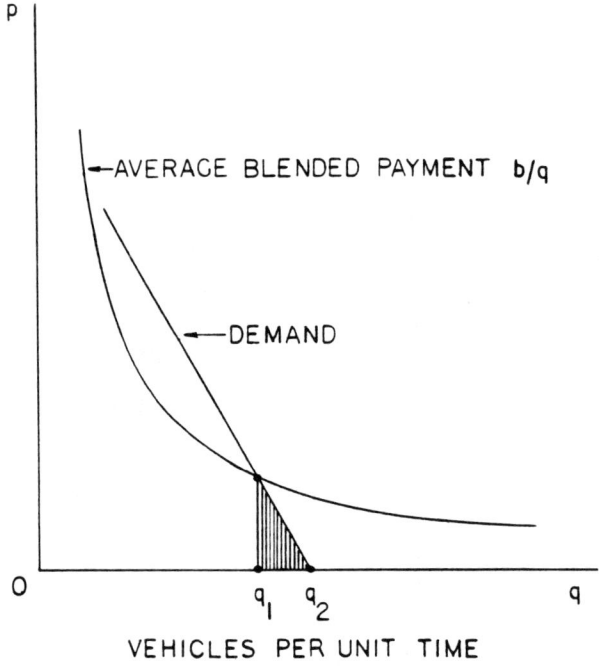

Figure 3P–7. Demand. Average Blended Payment, and Utility Loss

Here, since output-variable cost is zero, marginal cost is zero, and to set price to equal average blended payment implies a social cost equal to the shaded area, since all vehicles between q_1 and q_2 impose no cost but have positive utility.

Next, the annual painting cost is a time-incremental cost exhibiting a similar hyperbolic average relationship.

Now although painting is a time-incremental cost (while the construction amortization is only a time-variable *expenditure*), painting is not vehicle variable. So, as with construction, it would be inefficient to recover full cost by operating with $p = $ Avg.Ptg.Cost.

Next, surface wear is vehicle-related—the greater the traffic, the greater the damage repair cost. If vehicles are uniform, the average cost curve is shown in figure 3P–8 (enlarged scale):

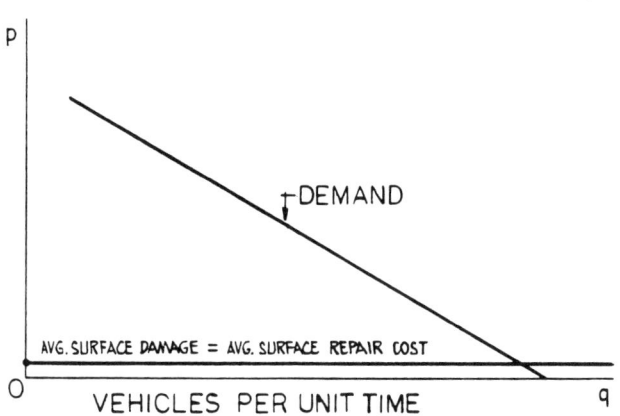

Figure 3P–8. Demand and Surface Repair Cost (Homogeneous Traffic)

Clearly, the average repair cost should be charged, unless collection costs are high in relation to repair costs, *and* demand is rather inelastic, so that dropping the toll entirely will not affect use and, hence, repair costs. In this case toll collection inputs would constitute an additional and unnecessary real resource cost.

Now we make the situation more realistic by dropping the homogenous traffic assumption. We must think in terms of equivalent traffic units (ETU); see problem 3.17:

1. Each vehicle is weighted by its AASHO coefficient;

2. Each weighted vehicle class volume is the number of vehicles of given weight multiplied by their AASHO coefficient;

3. These weighted classes are summed to yield the total equivalent traffic; and

4. this total is divided into the $1.2 million to derive a vehicle-variable cost.

It may still be the case that demand is inelastic, and it is not desirable to undertake the additional toll collection cost. In this case the whole cost should be borne by the (local) general public. However, the more diverse is traffic, the less reasonable is the assumption of general local benefit; rather, the effects are regional. As through traffic becomes more important, the more responsive to price is traffic likely to be. Therefore, it is desirable to impose a toll, even though this involves extra costs, but having installed the collection mechanism, it is also reasonable to collect the time-incremental cost (painting) on a discriminatory basis (undoubtedly, the passenger car equivalent traffic unit has a greater demand for this joint service than the big truck class and will pay more per ETU). But then, why not also impose a charge for the annual blended payment? A numerical example of discrimination is given in problem 7.4.

3.17. The AASHO Test was conducted to determine the relationship between axle weight and highway deterioration. Essentially, the damage coefficients ratio for two axle weights is approximately equal to the fourth power of their weight ratio. Suppose the traffic count in Ecalpon is determined to be (in miles per year):

Cars (2 tons)	20,000
2-axle medium truck (10 tons)	250,000
2-axle large truck (18 tons)	120,000

The annual road surface maintenance cost is $1,000,000. Determine how this should be recovered from the vehicle classes.

Solution

First, the calculation of traffic in equivalent traffic units is shown in table 3P-2.

Table 3P–2.
Calculation of Traffic Flows in Equivalent Traffic Units

	Number	Weight per Axle (tons)	Relative Weight	AASHO Damage Coefficient[a]	ETU 000s	%
Cars	20,000	1.0	1.0	1.0	40	.00
Medium trucks	250,000	5.0	5.0	625.0	312,500	.17
Large trucks	120,000	9.0	9.0	6561.0	1,574,640	.83
					1,887,180	1.00

[a]from ASSHO Road Test.
Price per ETU: $50,000/1,887,180,000 = $.000026
    Price per car: 2 × .000026 = $.000052 = .0052¢
    Medium truck: 2 × (.000026 × 625) = $.002350 = .235¢
    Large truck: 2 × (.000026 × 6561) = $.3412 = 34.12¢

In actual situations any axle configuration must be AASHO weighted more specifically: for example, cab axle, tandem axles, single axles; also, the load (whether full, part, or empty) must be considered.

3.18. Suppose police protection can be expressed in terms of police-officer-years per year. Henry and Sally constitute a two-person community. Their demand curves are

$$D_H: q_H = 2.5 - .1p; \qquad p_H = 25 - 10q,$$
$$D_S: q_S = 3 - .2p; \qquad p_S = 15 - 5q,$$

where q is the number of police-officer-years and p is the price in $1,000s. Determine the efficient level of police protection and the prices to be paid by Henry and Sally if it costs $20,000 per police-officer-year. (This community may buy noninteger units of police protection.) What would you call these payments?

Figure 3P-9. Police Demand: Sally, Henry, and Market

Solution

Demand is anoprosthetic so $p = p_H + p_S$. This gives us

$$p = \begin{cases} (25 - 10q) + (15 - 5q) & 0 \le q \le 2.5, \\ = 40 - 15q, & (\text{or } 2.5 \le p \le 40); \\ 15 - 5q, & 2.5 < q < 3, \\ & (\text{or } 0 \le p < 2.5). \end{cases}$$

$q(20) = 1.3, \quad p_H = 25 - 10(1.3) = 11.7, \quad p_S(1.3) = 8.3.$

Hence,

$$p = p_S + p_H = 11.7 + 8.3 = 20.$$

These contributions will be made annually (or prorated into shorter periods) and, hence, will be considered taxes. Moreover, it is usually desirable to combine these payments with others and collect them together to reduce collection costs.

3.19. Of course, police protection cannot be measured by the number of officers. For any given annual expenditure there is a hypersurface (the multidimensional analogue of a surface in space), representing trade-offs among officers, motorcycles, weapons, squad cars, laboratory and forensic equipment, and all the other inputs or dimensions of police protection, which cannot be accurately constructed. Indeed, we cannot even quantify the degree of protection—what are its units of measurement? Can you think of any way to graphically depict the demand for police protection?

Solution

Put dollars on the horizontal axis. But how will you express demand?

3.20. If you have convinced yourself of the futility of the last challenge, but still have to deal with the need to pay for police protection, how would you go about getting people to reveal their demands for this service? Can you improve upon the suggestions in the text (keying the annual charge to the house value)?

Solution

Other possibilities might include direct taxes on income, where income may reflect some aspect of demand for which wealth (measured by house value) fails, and other wealth taxes, although it is difficult to assess and administer such taxes. Family size may be another index of demand for police protection. In all such cases payments would be made as taxes, but this should not diminish our conviction that these taxes are made according to demand.

Pricing and Public-Sector Activities • 41

3.21. Ecalpon has a federal structure with central, state–province, and local government levels. A number of activities are listed below. For each, indicate whether the public sector should perform the activity, and if so, why; what level should perform it; and whether a full-cost recovery policy should be pursued.

1. An agricultural experimental station in one of the states.
2. A commuter train in one of the cities.
3. A bridge for one of the cities with little expected increase in traffic when
   a. there is little long-distance through traffic;
   b. 50 percent of the traffic is long-distance through traffic.
   Also see problem 4.4.
4. A community college in a poor province.
5. Provision of power by a regional power grid.

Solution

1. Since it is difficult to control the pirating and resale of information, it would be hard for a private firm to sell research information and cover its costs. This is insufficient reason for public performance, however, but there are other considerations which reinforce this concern. The research may be adopted only after many years of experimentation: while returns are eventually high, farmers might not implement the results without inducement (that is, subsidized provision) because of risk and/or monopoly position. Since the benefits accrue locally, the public agency should be locally oriented—the state or the province.

Now, it is true that the whole nation benefits through better, cheaper crops, but these benefits are reflected in market prices and, ultimately, in profits to growers. On the other hand, if the research is of general applicability (respecting soils, climate, crops), a case can be made for federal support.

2. This is a local community benefit. If the city is poor, *and* if this is the most efficient way to transfer income, it could be paid for at higher level. But this is not likely to be the case. If the situation of figure 3–1b prevails, an argument for state or provincial support can be made. In the general case it should be paid for by the community. Whether the entire cost, or just the nonisochronic elements, should be recovered from users depends on the anticipated network expansion. If no further expansion is even remotely foreseen, isochronic costs should not be recovered. If further expansion is foreseen—an addition every year or two—the entire cost should be recovered lest the

traffic levels be socially inefficient and give false signals about demand (recall figure 1–2).

Why do we couple the ideas of further expansion and false demand signals? If there is no further expansion, the community may be regarded as relatively settled in its habits, and demand for this service is probably fairly inelastic. A lower price resulting from excluding the isochronic cost component will not give a serious exaggeration of demand. If the city is growing rapidly, demand for the service will be more sensitive, and neglect of isochronic cost will exaggerate demand and overstimulate construction at the next stage beyond what is desirable. All of this must lead to overinvestment in commuter service to the detriment of other activities in the city. Of course, if as is unfortunately often the case, the city prevails on the higher governments (state or federal) for outside subsidies, the city will manage to provide these other activities, but some other, possibly poorer state, will do without.

3. a. The considerations are much the same as those in 2, and the local authority should pay. Here the incremental operating costs are likely to be much lower in relation to isochronic costs, however, and collection costs will comprise a relatively large component. This may obviate the desirability of imposing any charge in the case of the non-expanding network. If the bridge is part of a chain of communications links, however, the same considerations as in the dynamic situation of 2 obtain.

b. A higher level (state, regional, or even federal) should build it, although all costs should be recovered through user charges for the same dynamic considerations as above.

4. Presumably, the local community is also poor, so neither it nor the province can undertake it. A federal income distribution subsidy is justified.

5. Users of the grid should pay all costs, although the administration and financing may be discharged by a public-sector agency, such as an SOE. If the grid is in a poor region, an exception may be made with federal subsidies.

Bibliographic Note

The three-way classification of public-sector activity motives—stabilization, income distribution, economic efficiency—is usually associated with the name of Richard Musgrave, whose book remains a classic in the field of public finance. The concept of "public good" was given diagrammatic life by Bowen and subsequently endowed with mathematical rigor by Samuelson (1954), while Steiner (1957) was the first to employ the construct operationally to determine the allocation of joint costs between two users (a power generating facility, usually a private-sector enterprise). The expression "anoprosthetic," for vertically additive demand curves, was introduced by me in *Transportation Economics and Public Policy* to try to avoid the bias to which the expression "public good" was unavoidably subject. This book also summarizes *The AASHO Road Test* listed below. A good survey of many of the important issues in public economics is Steiner's 1969 paper in the U.S. JEC collection cited in chapter 1.

References

Abouchar, Alan. *Transportation Economics and Public Policy.* New York: Wiley-Interscience, 1977.

Bowen, Howard. *Toward Social Economy.* New York: Rinehard, 1948.

Musgrave, Richard. *The Theory of Public Finance.* New York: McGraw-Hill, 1959.

National Academy of Sciences. *The AASHO Road Test* (Proceedings of a Conference), Washington, D.C.: National Academy of Sciences–National Research Council, 1962.

Samuelson, Paul. "The Pure Theory of Public Expenditures," *Review of Economics and Statistics* (November 1954).

Steiner, Peter. "Peak Loads and Efficient Pricing." *The Quarterly Journal of Economics* (November 1957).

4
Shadow Values

A shadow value adjustment is an attempt to make prices or costs reflect more closely the true social cost or value of an output or input than does the market price. Applications in some areas have become standard, while in others, use of shadow prices or costs continues to provoke controversy. For example, national income accounting methodology routinely imputes a value to owner-occupied dwellings in computing both the expenditure and income sides of the main macroeconomic income measure. Values are also ascribed to many other activities which do not pass through the market, such as on-farm consumption of home-grown production. The particular procedures employed or values assigned in any given situation are open to dispute, but there is no question about whether such practice should be employed.

Other areas where shadow adjustments must be considered are (1) miscellaneous social-cost/private-cost discrepancies, especially in publicly provided services; (2) labor and wages; (3) fiscal distortions, especially sales taxes and tariffs; and (4) capital charges and discount rates.

Miscellaneous Discrepancies

Miscellaneous discrepancies between social costs and private costs, especially of publicly provided services, may constitute the most important field for shadow adjustment, although many such adjustments often go unrecognized in discussions of shadow prices. Thus, while the social cost/private cost conflict is most often cast, for example, in terms of failure to account for pollution or environmental degradation in the calculation of private strip mine coal costs, the high subsidies and/or cross subsidies to highway and other publicly provided transportation and other services represent a very large deviation between public and private costs. The case of highway transport has already been noted and represents one of the most serious discrepancies. But there are also discrepancies wherever user charges are subsidized. This is often the case in air transportation and other large-scale public-sector activities, whether by SOEs or by direct agency involvement.

The reasons vary for excluding part of the total social costs. Sometimes a policy is a historical legacy, possibly representing an attempt to distribute real income more equitably or to promote national cohesion. It may result from misapplication or microeconomic theory, attempting to translate the result of a simplified two-dimensional cost analysis to real world situations—the fixed-cost/variable-cost classification—which neglects opportunities to discriminate. Moreover, even if isochronic costs are included through depreciation, problems for cost recovery arise when there are unforeseen changes in technology or regional stagnation: while efficient pricing may justify the write-off of the residual book value in particular cases there is a risk that a pattern is established for depreciation in other public sector activities which are not so affected.

Another source of price departure from social cost is the use of historical, rather than replacement, cost (Problems 4.1 and 4.2). While the difficulty is, of course, generally known to economists and accountants, it is not usually thought of as an exercise in shadow price adjustment, although that is precisely what it is.

From the discussion of chapter 2 it is easy to see that the welfare-maximizing economist should do everything possible to promote more rational analysis of correctly defined costs. The fact that it is typically a public-sector organ to which these discrepancies relate does not necessarily simplify the task of instituting more rational cost analysis and making market prices actually reflect social costs: regulatory authorities may have some tradional views about the classification of sunk costs or about joint cost allocation; there may be widespread consumer resistance to implementation of replacement cost rather than acquisition cost; and so on.

The need for eliminating these distortions, rather than merely making shadow adjustments, is also emphasized by the need to have SOEs perform in consonance with national welfare maximization. Although it is easy to argue that the only important thing from the public-sector viewpoint is that input costs for projects under consideration correctly reflect social costs (and this could easily be done during the calculating process), this would not optimize activities of SOEs, which must compete commercially with private firms in such areas as transportation or energy, for example. The truth is that activities of most SOEs cannot be measured by the same rod as hospitals, for example, and commercial principles must therefore be relied upon, but prices and other rules of the game must be the same as for private firms.

Another frequently cited source of departure of private cost from social cost arises in the analysis of congestion, which is particularly important since public projects are often built as a reaction to congestion (Problem 4.3).

Labor and Wages

Labor and wages comprise one of the areas most often linked to discussion of shadow prices. Two issues are involved: (1) the valuation of labor as an input into a production process, and (2) the valuation of time which often relies on wages as the point of departure.

1. Prices of labor should reflect the opportunity costs of its use, that is, the sacrifice involved by putting it to the particular use in question rather than using it in its best alternative elsewhere in the economy. But, it is argued, given the frictions in the economy the wage does not represent the opportunity cost as it is supposed to do in pure theory. Minimum wages, union-negotiated wages, or other forms of administered wages, existing alongside high unemploment, cannot be taken to represent either the opportunity cost or the unemployed worker's valuation of his nonwork time, since it must be obvious that a worker would gladly work for something between zero and the administered wage, and it is unreasonable to think that no employer would find it profitable to employ him at something less than the minimum.

Sometimes the argument is overstated, since it is often true that the employed worker has skills the unemployed does not have, so the administered wage may then be a correct reflection of his productivity. Hence, this should be the wage used to price the input of workers who must move into a new project. However, we would not expect administered wages to reflect opportunity costs for all employed workers, and it would be wrong to include salaries of redundant workers in the base for user cost calculations.

In the class of miscellaneous social cost deviations from private cost, we emphasized the need to move private costs closer to the true social costs, but a similar policy cannot be urged here. Minimum wages are usually designed to redress income imbalances, and reducing or eliminating them would undo this important objective. Even if the wages of some workers exceed their opportunity cost, no gain would accrue from discharging them, since their salaries, or portions thereof, really constitute an income transfer. What we must do then is determine the amount involved and subtract it from the total wage bill to try to arrive at the correct price for the service, but the basic wage structure should certainly not be tampered with.

It is probably more important to resolve the pricing of workers now unemployed who will be drawn into active participation by the new project. Using the minimum wage might render unviable projects which could pass an economic efficiency test under a more realistic estimate of the opportunity cost, which may be very low, for employing them.

The problem can be resolved without explicit reference to the quandary if a national income type measure is used, as we will see in subsequent chapters. Evidently, the problem is most contentious in countries or regions of high secular unemployment. If we use national income methodology to measure benefits, labor costs will be considered as benefits rather than costs. Therefore, even if workers are paid the minimum wage, it is added to, not deducted from, other benefits. Since the minimum wage represents an effort to remedy income inequality, counting it as a benefit not only reduces the exaggeration of opportunity cost, but tends to incline decisions in favor of projects with high income redistributive potential if the actual market minimum wage is used. In low-unemployment economies, on the other hand, we should expect administered wages and opportunity costs to deviate less widely in the first place. This treatment also allows for special problems of high-unemployment sectors (ethnic, functional, or regional) in advanced economies (Problem 8.1).

2. The valuation of time often takes wages as its point of departure to determine the benefit of time savings. Time may be saved when it is an input into production, or when it is leisure. Both types of savings may be made with the same project—for example, a road between two points, or a better paved road permitting faster travel.

It seems clear that where the savings relate to time as input to production, it should be valued at the market wage, the assumption being that the worker's time saving will be reemployed directly into production. Clearly, moreover, it is the before-tax wage that should be used, since this represents the value of the time saving (in the first instance an increase in profit) to the firm.

The valuation of leisure time savings, however, remains controversial. While the after-income-tax wage, rather than the before-tax wage, seems appropriate if wages are to be used as the basis for valuation, it is not obvious that the wage is the correct basic concept in the first place. Two points militate against using the wage: first, even the wage may not correctly reflect the labor–leisure trade-off where large time savings are concerned, and, since workers must usually accept a job offer on an all-or-none basis, the wage may not even reflect the value of the first hour of leisure sacrificed. This is especially true for projects involving vacation commuting, where the hour saved may be on Saturday, a common enough type of decision requiring public-sector action—highways, bridges, ferries—but there is little reasonable alternative to the use of the wage to measure values, and, for short time intervals, it is probably the best procedure. The second point is that if project decision making is overcentralized, there will be an income-regressive bias towards projects in high-income regions, thus further maldistributing income. However, adherence to the public finance principles of chapter 3 will minimize this problem (Problem 4.4).

Fiscal Distortions

Fiscal distortions include (1) sales and excise taxes and (2) import duties. They should be treated in the following way.

1. Sales taxes (or excise taxes, which may be thought of as a highly specialized sales tax falling on a narrowly delimited commodity group) in principle represent an attempt to redistribute income indirectly by taxing the pur-

chase, rather than the consumer directly. Both sales and excise taxes are supposed to be progressive: thus, typically, sales taxes are imposed on consumer goods other than necessities such as most foods, while excise taxes are imposed on luxuries—the more luxurious the good, the higher the tax rate. They are not ordinarily construed to represent a resource cost. Therefore they should be omitted from the calculation of both benefits and costs. (Note that they are subtracted from Gross National Product when calculating Net National Income.) One note of caution, however: what passes for a sales tax may in essence represent a real resource cost. It is often the case that sales taxes are collected from all users of motor fuels—automobiles and trucks, gasoline and diesel. Even if there is a specifically designated road user charge, that for trucks is usually too low to cover the warranted user charge, as estimated on the basis of true damage coefficients and modest allocation of joint (including isochronic) components. Hence, to compensate partly or wholly for this, sales taxes on truck fuel must be regarded as a true cost, together with the specifically designated user charge. A saving of fuel input should then be valued as the sum of the fuel purchase price (including specifically designated road user tax), and the saving of the sales taxes since these savings represent a reduction in damage imposed on the system. But the coincidence—or failure to coincide—of user payments and warranted user charges must be verified in individual cases.

2. Import duties are a second fiscal instrument complicating the determination of true social costs. The view is often expressed that border prices (net c.i.f. prices for imports and f.o.b. port prices for exports) represent the costs and gains in terms of foreign exchange, which is one of the scarce factors for any economy, but especially for those trying to develop. It has been pointed out, in opposition, that these prices represent the relative factor endowments (including labor skills) existing at a particular time, and it is precisely the objective of development to change these: if world relationships, reflected through border prices, are to be used, such changes will never be achieved, and an underdeveloped country will be doomed to remain so.

We believe that the treatment of the duty should depend on the purpose of the duty and the end use of the good—whether input or output. Let us see why.

Any particular duty may be imposed for income distribution or efficiency objectives. Even if the stated purpose is "revenue raising," it is clear that, since imports are not typically consumed by the poor, the higher-income groups will contribute disproportionately to this revenue, so an income distribution motive can be inferred. (Of course, if the revenues are to be spent totally on high-income groups, redistribution will not in fact occur, but the problem then is the expenditure, rather than the collection, side.)

Duties imposed for efficiency purposes are designed to encourage domestic production and import substitution or to discourage external debt.

Ideally, an efficiency-based duty will just exceed the value of the domestic production cost disadvantage: a lower duty will not encourage import substitution, and a higher duty will encourage inefficient substitution—either production in the wrong conditions or poor control over input costs.

Now, one problem in analyzing duties is that, for any specific efficiency-based duty, one can never know whether it meets the conditions just stated: in general, it is difficult to know in advance of an undertaking what the domestic cost will be following the learning period, so it is not possible to judge whether the duty is a correctly set efficiency mechanism. Moreover, it may even be difficult to know whether the duty is designed for distribution or efficiency objectives in the first place. For example, a duty on a luxury sports car is clearly a distribution-related duty, since sports car import substitution is not remotely feasible. But what about a midsized sedan? Furthermore, duties may be imposed on categories which are narrowly defined, but may, nonetheless, be broad enough to include inputs as well as outputs. "Four-wheeled powered vehicles" may constitute a rubric on the tariff schedule, perhaps a carryover from earlier days when all such vehicles were pleasure cars, but now this category may include pickup trucks or special purpose production vehicles. Even taxis are an input rather than an output, although there is less likely to be a need to consider them in project evaluations (Problem 4.5).

Table 4-1 shows the four possible configurations: duties designed for distribution and efficiency imposed on inputs and outputs. Illustrative items are provided, and the recommended treatment is indicated in each cell at which the characteristics intersect.

We have assumed throughout that the duties are not designed to compensate for undervalued exchange rates. Duties that are designed for such purposes, or, for that matter, differentiated exchange rate premiums, can also be introduced into the analysis. Usually it will be the case that intermediate capital goods for production have relatively lower foreign exchange prices, while consumption goods (including components for local assembly) are imported at higher foreign exchange costs. Can the lower capital goods costs associated with preferential exchange rates be taken to reflect the government's preference for speedy development? If so, they should be used to calculate the benefit of a project.

Now, of course, governments do not publish lists of motives for particular duties or expectations about type of use—final or intermediate. So, how can we tell if tariffs or exchange rate discounts and premiums correctly reflect the government's assessment of the needs and pace of development? This question must be answered in the local context: if there is extensive local debate on the economics of development, and if tariffs and exchange rates are relatively stable, we may assume provisionally that exchange rates, import duties, prices, and development objectives are consistent. Rates which

Table 4–1
Examples of Treatment of Import Duties for Shadow Adjustments

	Purpose of Duty	
Use of Import	*Income Distribution*	*Economic Efficiency*
As consumption good	A luxury automobile. No problem arises since there is no need to be concerned from the viewpoint of project evaluation.	A midsized or midpriced sedan, a compact model automobile, bicycles, plastic containers. If we use the national income approach to benefit measurement and calculate it from the income side, we will be calculating the cost of production in terms of wages, capital, and net intermediate goods—net value added. If the import duty does correctly reflect the domestic cost disadvantage (following the break-in period), the income side of the accounts should equal the expenditure side of the accounts calculated in terms of import-inclusive landed prices. To be on the safe side, we should approach the project from the income side and tariffs will not enter. Indeed, to the extent that the two disagree it could be argued that the efficiency-related duty is incorrectly set.
As intermediate good	A jeep, pickup, or dump truck to be used in connection with an irrigation project. The duty is imposed on the class of four-wheeled vehicles since, historically, there was no need to separate special purpose vehicles since they constituted such a small total. Therefore, the duty does not represent a real resource cost and should be subtracted from the price of the input. But to the extent that a duty is desired for efficiency purposes, some duty should be included. See column at right.	Polyethylene pipe, steel extrusions, or small trucks which could be manufactured domestically. Duty should be included in the price of the input since using it represents a reduction in the use of domestic substitutes, actual or potential.

bounce around in random fashion, however, cannot be assumed to be efficient, since productivity differentials are not so volatile.

Capital

Capital theory is one of the most difficult areas of economic analysis and surely one of the most important, as it deals with the allocation and optimization of embodied labor. While this issue is the subject of chapter 5, it arises naturally in a discussion of shadow prices also, and we will introduce the problems here.

One major obstacle to analysis is caused by the abundance of relevant terms and concepts. Many of these concepts are functions whose value depends on some factor—for example, marginal productivity of capital—which, at any time, reflects incremental output attainable for the next investment dollar and thus varies as a function of the investment level. Others are equilibrium values which depend on some of the functions—the social rate of discount which is equal to the marginal productivity of capital and, at the same time, to the social rate of time preference. Thus, the social rate of discount and marginal productivity of capital cannot be taken as alternatives, as is sometimes done; they are different concepts, but in equilibrium they have the same value.

A particularly vexatious notion is the "true rate of interest." Some commentators seem to mean by this that correct discount rate for society to use in project calculations. But it is easily confused with the term "real rate of interest," which is the difference between the market rate of interest on any type loan and the rate of inflation. Thus, there are as many real rates of interest as there are financial instruments.

The main terms and concepts to deal with include the following:

Borrowing interest rate:	Amount that a borrower must pay per dollar borrowed (for bank or bond loans).
Prime rate:	In principle, the borrowing rate relevant to "prime" corporate accounts, presumed to be least likely to default. However, many "prime" customers pay less, or more, and of course the rate may vary with maturity.
Real rate of interest:	Rate of interest minus the rate of inflation; may refer to any interest category (prime rate, treasury bill rate, Aaa bond rate, and so on.

Central bank (discount) rate:	Rate which the central bank charges commercial banks for short-term loans.
Rate of discount:	A factor which is to be applied, on a compound basis, to reduce future earnings or costs to make them equivalent to money today.
Individual (social) rate of time preference:	Rate at which an individual (society) is willing to sacrifice a unit of present consumption for a unit of future consumption. It varies with consumption and income levels.
Marginal productivity of capital:	Rate of increase in future production generated by sacrificing a unit of consumption today. It varies with investment level.
Social role of discount:	Rate for discounting projects in the public sector, simultaneously equal to the marginal productivity of capital and the intertemporal social rate of time preference.

Additional complications are caused by thinking in terms of total income—total output of goods and services, including investment goods—rather than consumption alone.

In view of the variety of terms and concepts, it is neither surprising nor objectionable that many economists have written about introducing shadow prices for capital, but often the positions are reconcilable, as with the social rate of discount mentioned above.

As one particular example of difficulty, consider the use of the borrowing rate charged to a public-sector agent whose bond interest payment is exempt from federal income tax, as is the case with subfederal public agencies in the United States. Here a nominal rate equal to half the prime rate would, to a lender in the 60-percent federal income tax bracket, be worth 25 percent more than an investment paying the prime rate. That is, if 6 percent is the rate on a tax-exempt municipal, and 12 percent is the rate on the non-tax-exempt bond of a "prime" corporation, the return of $60 on the $1,000 tax-exempt bond is the equivalent of $.4r$, where r, the equivalent rate, is equal to 15 percent. Which, if any, of these three rates should be used for the project evaluation, and how should it be used, (for example, as a dicounting instrument or as an actual price paid on borrowed funds)?

54 • *Project Decision Making in the Public Sector*

Yet another issue is the treatment of public-sector revenues which are not borrowed—income taxes, user charges, and sales and excise taxes. Here the absence of an interest payment certainly does not mean that the use of capital should be regarded as free, but if the interest rate were accepted as the price of capital, a zero charge must be imposed, since it is a fact that no interest is being paid.

These issues can be illuminated only after a deeper investigation into the nature of capital productivity and the measurement of benefits with which we begin part II.

Problems

4.1 The Ecalpon Export Rail Line (EERL) was built in 1975 at a cost of $10 million (breaking down 40–60 between isochronic and variable or consumable capital inputs). The facility, originally paid for by its parent company Ecalpon Iron Ore out of retained earnings, was built to carry ore to the coast for export, but an evenly balanced, two-way traffic subsequently developed. EERL is depreciating the capital investment on a straight-line, twenty-five year term, this being the expected life of the rolling stock. An overall annual inflation rate of 35 percent has prevailed throughout the economy so that the general price level in 1983 is eleven times as high as it was in 1975. How will this affect the demand for rail transportation on the EERL?

Solution

The general traffic demand curve will shift to the right, with prices being expressed in nominal terms. (If the cargo mix is the same as the market basket for which the inflation index has been calculated, the shipping demand curve should relate the same quantities to the old prices multiplied by 11.) Since the demand for ore shipment depends on the world market price for ore, which will have risen more or less, it will also shift to the right, but not necessarily by the same proportion.

4.2 Some voices are arguing that EERL should raise its rates in line with inflation while others are heard arguing for the low rates as an impetus for development. What policy would you advocate and why?

Solution

The 60 percent of initial investment, properly depreciated, should be adjusted by the inflation factor, which we presume to reflect the change in replacement cost of these capital assets. (If we know precisely the replacement cost, it should be used.) Since ore and general cargo demand intensities may have changed in relative terms, there may have to be a change in the allocation of the output-variable joint costs, such as ballast cleaning or locomotive movement. If, as here, it is merely generalized inflation that we are dealing with, and the cost was being fully recovered before inflation set in, an upward-revalued basic capital stock can continue to be recovered subsequently through similarly adjusted rail rates. Also, as we have stressed repeatedly, given so many dimensions of demand (direction, cargo type, and vehicle type) it should be possible to institute, in the first place, full-cost recovery by discriminating, without inducing any welfare loss.

4.3 Suppose there has been no inflation, but traffic has grown rapidly, and the line is congested to the extent that each additional carload causes a sharp slowdown in movement, thus raising the inventory costs of other shippers as well as the marshalling yard operation of EERL. Suppose that the private cost per ton is given by

$$c(q) = \begin{cases} 1.0, & 0 < q \leq 100, \\ .0012q^2 - .0018q - 10.82, & 100 < q. \end{cases}$$

This is the private cost, or average social cost, which confronts each individual user. (The shipping time is longer and the railroad must pass along extra private costs.) The increment to social cost imposed by the user on account of causing slowdowns for all other shippers is the derivative of total cost ($TC = q \cdot c$) with respect to q, for example,

$$MSC = \frac{dTC}{dq} = \begin{cases} 1.0 & 0 < q \leq 100, \\ .0036q^2 - .0036q - 10.82, & 100 < q. \end{cases}$$

The situation is shown in figure 4P–1.

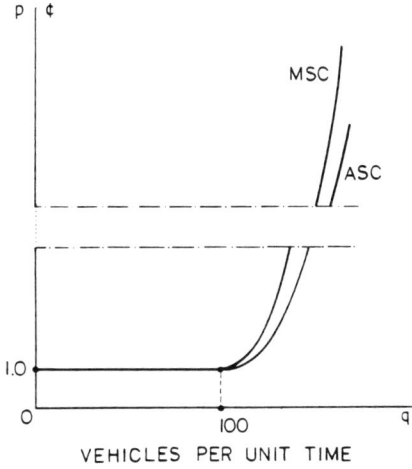

Figure 4P–1. Basic Congestion Analysis

Suppose the demand is given by $q(p) = 10{,}000 - 100p$. What price should be charged each ton of freight?

Solution

The essence of congestion is that people do not pay for the costs they inflict on others, and so they are inefficiently induced to partake of the activity—highway travel, air transportation, or rail. It was once thought—and even now sometimes in popular discussion it is argued that—congestion is optimally self-regulating, because when things slow down and travel becomes more costly, any entrant must pay the higher cost, and unless he values the service at least that much, he will not enter. But as economists have long argued, and as this numerical example shows, this is not the case: each shipper is concerned only with his own costs, which, while higher than those over the noncongested activity range (between 0 and 100), are less than the costs he imposes on society. The optimal activity level and congestion charge are determined from MSC and ASC as follows.

We equate price and MSC (anticipating that optimal activity will exceed 100) and find (after first finding the inverse demand function)

$$p = 100 - .01q = .0036q^2 - .0036q - 10.82 = MSC$$

or

$$.0036q^2 + .0064q - 110.82 = 0,$$

whence $q = 177$ (rounding). Here, $ASC = 26.4$; $MSC = 101.3 = p$.

Thus, the congestion premium is $MSC - ASC = (101.3 - 26.4) = 74.9$¢ per ton for the journey.

The relevance of shadow prices or costs arises here in the inability to incorporate the congestion control premium (the difference between MSC and ASC at optimal output) into the price paid by each user. Thus, it is tempting to say that the true benefit from expanding the line capacity is given by MSC at the present activity level, but we must be careful because this is the gross benefit only of the last unit performed. For each of the preceding units, MSC is lower. Thus we would not use a single value, but, if you like, a shadow function and look at something like the integral under the MSC curve. I say "something like" advisedly, because, of course, the curve is quite an abstraction, and what we must do is simply add up the various resource inputs which are to be spared by eliminating congestion or reducing it to some specified level.

The theory of congestion derives most of its relevance and value from the instructional insights it provides rather than its ability to prescribe clear answers to problems of congestion. It shows unequivocally that the burden imposed by the marginal congestor exceeds his own cost, and this is valuable knowledge. But the curves cannot be easily inferred; indeed, since the congestion imposed is not only a function of a person's point of entry, but also of his own characteristics, the MSC curve cannot be easily drawn. For example, the congestion cost associated with the 100th vehicle in the traffic stream depends on the type of vehicle and the length of the trip.

In sum, congestion theory is valuable because it reminds us that one's own private costs may not correctly reflect the average cost of a phenomenon. But we must recognize the other part of congestion theory as well—that the imposed cost will fall for inframarginal units, and these are the costs which must be used. But, finally, since the cost function cannot be easily specified for most transport activities, we must go out and measure the resource costs themselves. These costs will, of course, include time.

4.4 Ecalpon is a federal state, and its constituent states vary greatly in average income—$5,00 per hour in A-state and $2.50 per hour in Z-state. This is partly due to different price levels which have developed historically and partly to higher labor demand in A-state. An income transfer system is now in place through unemployment insurance and supplementary welfare grants. A bridge is being contemplated in each state and there is enough money for only one. In either state the same number of leisure travel hours will be saved. There are no commercial users. How should the decision be made?

Solution

Since Ecalpon is now possessed of an income transfer mechanism, there is a presumption that the poor are being sufficiently cared for even though there is no explicit interstate transfer device. Welfare payments keyed to income will themselves work to reduce interregional income differentials (unless all the poorest people are in the same state with the richest people, in which case we cannot speak of interstate differences). Furthermore, there seems to be little in its technology or scope that would commend a bridge for consideration as an income transfer device in the first place. The situation might change if the bridge enables people in Z-state to commute to more productive and better paying jobs but this is not the case. So the choice must be made strictly on efficiency grounds. In the absence of a better measure of time value, we may use the wage, which is higher in A-state, and, since the number of hours saved is the same in the two states, the total value of the benefit will be twice as high in A-state. But if the investment is to be made centrally (out of general purpose tax revenues, for example), income inequality will be exacerbated through the net transfer to A-state. This seems undesirable. Moreover, since the proposal to use the wage as a basis for time valuation may be problematic to begin with, A-state runs the greater risk of exaggerating the total annual benefit if it is to be paid for by outsiders. If A-state truly does believe that the wage represents the value of time savings, however, it should undertake the investment through its own resources, either through a local tax or local bond issue. Whether A-state should pay out of general tax revenues, with subsequent recovery from users of only the subsequently time- or traffic-variable costs, or whether all costs should be recovered from the users may depend on the different administration costs of the alternatives, together with considerations of whether almost all of the state, or only the local populace will use the facility (compare Problem 3.21, 3a).

4.5 Ecalpon imports baby strollers with a 40 percent tariff. A private firm wants to enter the business and believes it can produce them at a price 35–40 percent higher than the imported price, net of duty. There is high secular unemployment in the country. The firm wants to undertake production, but it requires a government loan. The government may have to choose among different applicants planning to produce different products. What stroller price should be used in calculating the benefits of this project?

Solution

The tariff-inclusive price should be used. The wholesale price of the strollers to be manufactured will be approximately equal to this price, which will break down into wages and profits of the firm, all items which will be treated as benefits in our national income type benefit calculations. Note, if the 35 percent higher production cost already includes the normal return for the firm, it is to be expected that the wholesale price will be driven down to this level, so 1.35 times the landed net price should be used. However, given the roughness of such calculations, it is as well to take the duty-inclusive price on the grounds that the entrepreneur himself is in the best position to judge his private costs and all we can be confident of is that he believes he can sell the strollers for no more than 1.4 times the landed net price, but possibly that much.

Notice, however, the similarity to the example in the northeast cell of table 4–1. There it was reasoned that calculating the GNP contribution from the income side—wages and salaries, profits—would circumvent the need to consider the output prices and the tariff-shadow price issue.

Bibliographic Note

There is a large literature on shadow prices, although very little of it is devoted to what we call miscellaneous deviations between price and cost stemming from incorrectly applied economic principles in pricing the public sector. A good overview and classification of many of the issues is the book by Little and Mirrlees; one of their main tenets is the use of world prices as the main guide to valuation, leaving enough flexibility, however, to accommodate certain government preferences for economic development and foreign exchange (pp. 105–114 are extracted as a reading in Layard). The articles by McKean, Sen, and Harrison and Quarmby in Layard, and those by Margolis and Haveman in U.S. JEC are also good analyses of various issues, including foreign exchange, duties, labor, and time. Some empirical studies reported on in these volumes which assign shadow values include those by Foster and Beasly on time savings from subway construction (in Munby), Mack and Meyers on the value of recreation time by income class (in Dorfman), Fromm on time savings value in civil aviation (in Dorfman), and Weisbrod (in Layard) and Marglin (in Maas) on income distribution shadow weights. (All of the foregoing are cited in full in chapter 1, Bibliographic note.)

Price imputations for national income components are described in varying degrees of detail in the publications of the U.S. Department of Commerce and Statistics Canada.

A large literature also exists on shadow prices of capital (see, for example, Feldstein, Sen, Marglin, and Harberger, cited in chapter 1).

Part II
Decision Criteria

5
Comparing Benefits over Time

We turn to the specific decision rules. We first must stress once again that not all potential public-sector investment activities can be reduced to similar terms and compared with one another to determine the optimal set of investments in any given year. Different sectors may require special approaches. The aim of the analyst, then, should be to investigate and ensure their consistency and the *tendency* of each approach to develop rules, including prices, which promote an investment pattern consistent with efficiency and the nation's distributional objectives.

To put it another way, what some have viewed as the main rationalizing force for public-sector investment—cost-benefit analysis—cannot be applied to all projects in the public sector because the economy is simply too complex. In particular, it cannot be applied in isolation from the question of the source of project financing, since very often it is the actual or prospective ability of the users themselves to cover the costs of the project that will indicate its potential value. Of course, this does not rule out the possibility that, within the scope of the local public sector, financing may be based partly on general tax revenues and partly on user payments for services currently rendered.

Within cost-benefit theory itself, the main challenges have been to decide how to measure net benefits. For example, one specific problem has been to decide how to add together benefits of very different nature for an irrigation project, say: the increased agricultural output can go through the market, or, if it is a subsistence agriculture project, it may have a readily identifiable market counterpart from which prices can be inferred and values imputed. But the improved environmental ambience which may follow from the project does not have a market, or readily identifiable, value. Local housing opportunities will be affected. Similar problems affect the consideration of time savings for a new airport or road. We will argue that the much espoused criterion of consumer surplus is defective, since it is used only in certain types of project and completely neglected in others, the implication being that there is no consumer surplus in many activities, which is inconsistent with the principle of downward sloping demand curves. Moreover, it assumes stability of demand curves, but the very nature of many projects causes demand relationships to change very substantially. This can bias investment selection badly.

A second important problem is to decide on the nature of, not to speak of the numerical value of, the discount factor used to reduce benefits occurring at different dates to an equivalent basis, the subject of this chapter.

Assume all possible projects which can be evaluated and decided upon have been assigned a subscript and their economic impacts have been analyzed. Assume also that no two projects are mutually exclusive, that is, for any possible application only the best project is chosen for closer examination: the best combination of route, pipeline diameter, and compressor technology for the exploitation of some particular oil field, for example. Let I_i denote the investment expenditure for project i, R_{it} the net return of project i in year t, and $R_{i0} = -I_i$ the net benefit in year zero (for simplicity we assume that the project can be built and introduced within a single year). The problem before us is to decide how to compare returns in the second and successive years with the investment expenditure—both the acquisition of the output-variable or consumable capital goods and the isochronic costs.

Traditionally, two criteria are used: the net discounted value, or present worth, and the internal rate of return. Neither is perfect or complete under all circumstances, and judicious use requires a thorough exposure to their essential features and limitations. Often a third criterion is also applicable—the ability of an investment to generate income sufficient to repay the loan and the interest. This is especially appropriate for projects of SOEs or projects financed by revenue bonds.

Net Present Value

For any individual, as long as there are no borrowing constraints, the optimal investment rule is to invest all projects for which the net present value is positive. The net present value of project i is defined as

$$NPV_i = \sum_{t=0}^{T_i} R_{it}(1+d)^{-t},$$

where T_i is the project life, d is the discount factor, R_{it} is the net return in year t, and the zeroth year is the year during which the investment is made (Problem 5.1). Assume for (undeceptive) simplification that the investment is made instantaneously and there is no return in year zero. Writing $-I_i$ for R_{i0}, NPV_i takes the form

$$\sum_{t=1}^{T_i} R_{it}(1+d)^{-t} + R_{i0} \quad \text{or} \quad \sum_{t=1}^{T_i} R_{it}(1+d)^{-t} - I_i,$$

and the corresponding decision rule is to invest in any project for which

$$\sum_{t=1}^{T_i} R_{it}(1+d)^{-t} > I_i.$$

The discount factor d is the rate at which money can be borrowed and reinvested (provisionally assumed to be equal for simplicity).

This rule can be derived in two ways. First, let d be the minimal rate of return to investment. Now, $\sum_{t=1}^{T_i} R_{it}(1+d)^{-t} > I_i$ means that

$$\sum_{t=1}^{T_i} R_{it}(1+d)^{-t} = X_{i1} + X_{i2} + \cdots + X_{iT_i} = I'_i > I_i,$$

with $X_{it} = R_{it}(1+d)^{-t}$. That is, we can think of dividing up the total discounted present value, which we denote I'_i, into annual components X_{it}. But since investment may be made at a rate of return equal to $1 + d$ per year each of these components X_{it} may be invested for t years to yield $X_{it}(1+d)^t$. But this is precisely the return in year t since

$$X_{it}(1+d)^t = R_{it}(1+d)^{-t}(1+d)^t = R_{it}.$$

Therefore, this means that the dollar volume I_i is acquiring more than it might be expected to acquire if invested elsewhere in the economy—I'_i dollars, in fact.

A rather different approach, which will also help us to understand the NPV–IRR controversy, is the following. The return in year t can be reinvested to yield a return of $(1+d)R_{it}$. The process can be repeated in the next year. This can then be reinvested right up to, and including, year T_i, so that it will earn $(1+d)^{T_i - t}R_{it}$ from the time it is earned until the end of the investment life. The total returns then will be

$$\sum_{t=1}^{T_i} R_{it}(1+d)^{T_i - t} = \sum_{t=1}^{T_i} R_{it}(1+d)^{T_i}(1+d)^{-t}$$

$$= (1+d)^{T_i} \sum_{t=1}^{T_i} R_{it}(1+d)^{-t}.$$

Meanwhile, the investment I_i could generate at least $(1+d)^{T_i} I_i$ by the end of the period if invested in any project with this life at the rate of return d. Therefore we should not want to invest in any project unless

$$(1 + d)^{T_i} \sum_{t=1}^{T_i} R_{it}(1 + d)^{-t} > (1 + d)^{T_i} I_i,$$

or

$$\sum_{t=1}^{T_i} R_{it}(1 + d)^{-t} > I_i,$$

which is our original rule as first stated.

The foregoing analysis assumes that the individual or firm can borrow and invest without restriction. We also implicitly assumed that he could borrow and lend at the same rate d. It is easy to take account of violations of this last assumption, and we would then conclude with the criterion

$$\sum_{t=1}^{T_i} R_{it}(1 + d)^{-t} > \left(\frac{1 + d_b}{1 + d_l}\right)^{T_i} I_i$$

as the decision rule, where the subscripts b and l have their obvious meanings.

What has been thus far said readily extends to the entire economy, although for a planner to simultaneously inspect all projects would be a more difficult problem.

We have assumed unlimited access to credit markets, but if, as is usually the case, the borrower—individual, firm, or economy—must sacrifice part of the present consumption rather than borrow without limit, we must analyze the borrower's willingness to make such a sacrifice. This leads to a criterion which equates the marginal productivity of capital and the marginal rate of substitution or rate of time preference in consumption. However, as derived in economic theory, the frame of reference is two periods, and extension to an arbitrary number of periods requires that the rate d also be the rate at which the earnings can be reinvested in the future. Moreover, it is traditionally established only in terms of consumption that can be diverted to investment in order to produce consumption during the next period, but many of the project benefits will not have this character—time savings in travel, for example. Furthermore, since many of the projects will generate nonconsumption outputs such as intermediate capital goods or services, the analysis must be extended beyond the consumption sector alone. We will proceed in stages to extend the rule.

Suppose that the possibilities for consumption this year (C_0) and next (C_1) are fully known and the economy has access to the international capital market, which is willing to lend money at rate r. The economy can then commit part of tomorrow's consumption to pay for imports today and consume more this year than next. The possibilities are shown as a consumption frontier in figure 5–1 (the smooth curve). Of course, for a Crusoe economy which depends on its own internal resources, the frontier could not extend south of the 45° line, since such an economy could not trade off goods that it would not have until tomorrow for goods to consume today. Moreover, the curve would undoubtedly double back as C_0 became very small, since, below some level of consumption today, the population would be too weak to enjoy tomorrow what it might otherwise be able to produce. But we will assume that the economy is relatively open and does have access to foreign capital.

The smooth curve in figure 5–1 is really the smoothing out of a polygonal graph which shows the successive increments in next year's consumption that could be achieved by sacrificing some of this year's consumption. The projects are ordered so that the sacrifice in consumption for the one with the highest rate of return (that is, the one for which $-\Delta C_i/\Delta C_0$ or $|\Delta C_1/\Delta C_0|$ is highest) is placed furthest out on the C_0 axis. The others are then placed in order of decreasing return. The slope of the smoothed consumption frontier is dC_1/dC_0, which is negative. That is, the slope at point P is the slope of the tangent line LL, which we denote s. Defining capital as the consumption sacrifice of this year which can then be used to increase consumption next year, we may think of the absolute value of this rate of transformation as the marginal productivity of capital (MPK) at any level of investment: a sacrifice of one unit of consumption today will permit the economy ($MPK - 1$) extra unit of consumption tomorrow. The relationship between the MPK for public-sector projects and the rate of interest is explored in Problem 5.2.

To speak of *the* marginal productivity of capital in the economy requires that we select a single value from the range of possible values. The marginal productivity of capital is defined as the differential gain in next year's consumption at the point at which the last unit of consumption is sacrificed. If we knew the whole curve, we could tell, at any level of investment, what the productivity of the next unit to be sacrificed was. But the viewpoint of the investment decision makers in practice is the other way around: given a marginal productivity of investment norm, let all projects be undertaken which yield a return at least equal to that productivity. The decision rule stated at the outset is a way of casting the problem mathematically. If we assume that the frontier does not change over the next T_i years, the decision rule stated at the outset can be seen to fulfill just this requirement if the discount rate d is equal to MPK. How do we determine a single value for MPK?

To take account of the economy's preferences, we introduce a community indifference curve for consumption this year and next. It is shown in figure 5–2 together with the consumption possibility frontier from figure 5–1. If the community has access to the international financial market, it can operate at

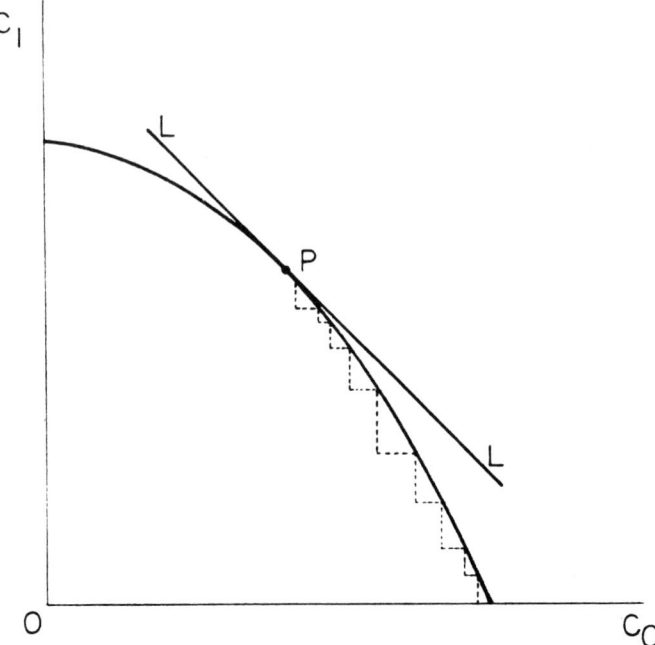

Figure 5–1. Two Period Consumption Frontier

consumption levels defined by the coordinates of point A, the point of tangency of the highest indifference curve and the consumption frontier, trading off this year's consumption for next year's at the rate given by the slope of the tangent line.

This analysis is adequate for the investment decision principles in the two-period situation when goods can be traded without hindrance. But four questions arise when we seek to apply it to the typical project evalution:

1. What happens when we move to the multiperiod framework?
2. Can it be used to evaluate projects generating consumption-like benefits, such as time savings, which may represent a very important objective of a project, but, being nonmarketable, cannot be exchanged through a market to increase future consumption?
3. Can it be used for projects in which an important benefit takes the form of nonconsumption, such as employment of otherwise idle workers in road maintenance in areas for which a LTFCR user charge policy is being pursued (whether justifiable or not)? The problem here arises from the fact that subsidized user charges imply that the final measured consumption prices do not reflect all benefits.

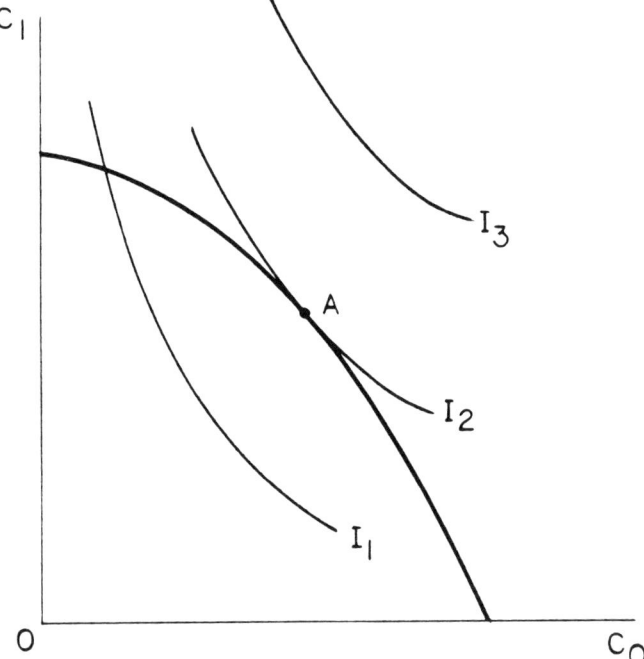

Figure 5-2. Two Period Consumption Equilibrium

4. How do we know the marginal rate of substitution for consumption, that is, the slopes of the community indifference map?

None of these problems has an easy answer, but a review of the important difficulties will enable us to proceed reasonably in various applications.

1. For the multiperiod analysis our net benefit criterion implicitly assumes that production possibilities and tastes will remain as they are today. While these curves will undoubtedly change their shapes somewhat, it is probably reasonable to assume that the resulting tangency will not change very much from today's. The same could be said about future years up through year T_i. However, if there is evidence to the contrary, a discount rate depending on time can be introduced, but this may require assumptions which may be as far off as any assumption about constant MPK.

2. Some benefits will not only be nonmarketable, but they will not lend themselves to trading over time. Suppose a contemplated project will lead to a total community time saving of m dollars per year. Suppose the investment generating this value is the one at C_0' in Figure 3-3a. In this case the consumption frontier takes a jump at C_0', since, when we undertake this project, we make a sacrifice today but get back next year, not only an increase in market consumption, but an increase in nonmarket consumption equal to m,

70 • Project Decision Making in the Public Sector

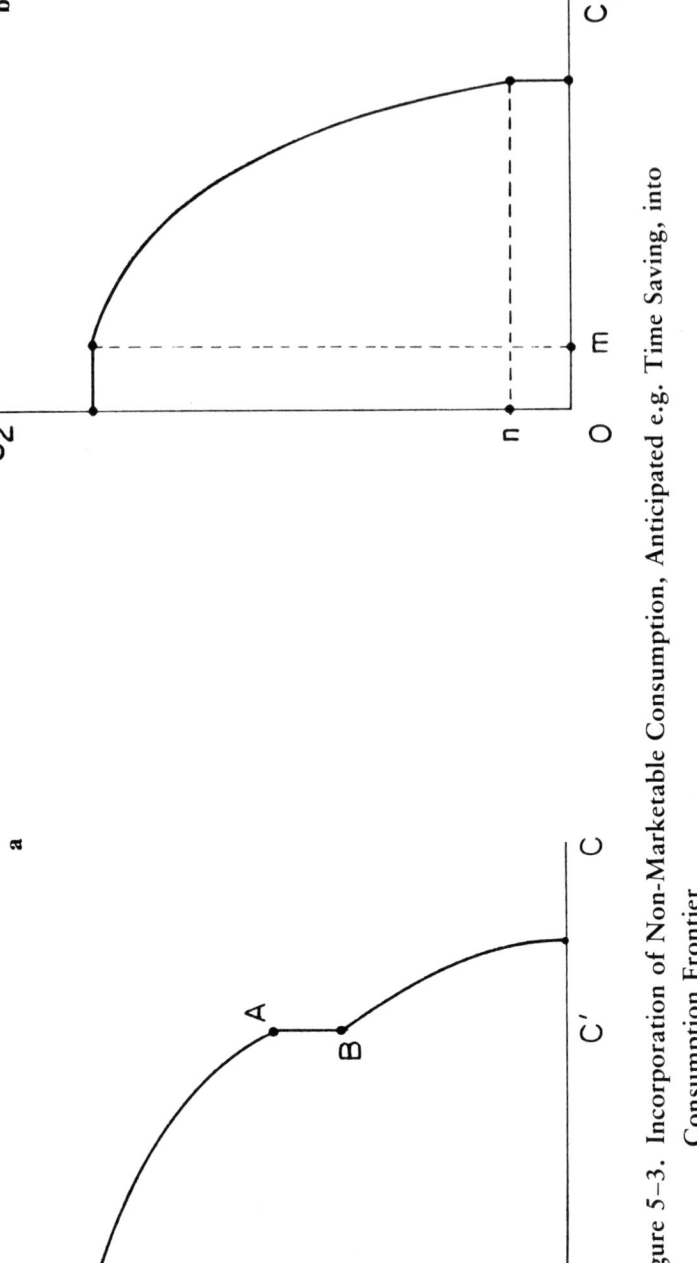

Figure 5–3. Incorporation of Non-Marketable Consumption, Anticipated e.g. Time Saving, into Consumption Frontier

shown by the line segment *AB*. Clearly this presents a problem for the theory of two-period optimization because of the nondifferentiability of the frontier. But this may not be serious, since, when we look beyond the second year, we see that the frontier has both horizontal and vertical flat portions, which may be regarded as defining the maximum range over which a "freely acquired" service is possible. That is, we can get any amount of value of period-one consumption up to *m* dollars without sacrificing any period-zero consumption; and similarly the first *m* dollars of period-zero consumption do not impinge on period-one consumption. This is shown in figure 5–3b.

But again, the constancy of the marginal productivity of investment over time beyond the second year must be explicitly assumed, and it must also be assumed that it will be equal to the marginal rate of product substitution in consumption to yield a single social rate of time preference. This may or may not be reasonable. Indications to the contrary, if they can be determined, should be built in to the net benefit criterion by allowing the discount rate to depend on time.

3. The analysis so far has been restricted to consumption. But many of the projects to be undertaken will contribute to investment output rather than consumption—construction of a reservoir, for example, which will not be consumed in the next period but over many decades. The reservoir is an example of a capital facility producing consumption goods, but a coal mine producing fuel for a steel smelter is not. Moreover, there are activities such as road maintenance which often fail to be included in the user charge base in the first place and so do not show up in final consumer goods prices, even though maintenance represents an important economic activity, one we would like to count as a benefit if the workers are otherwise unemployed, since the act of drawing workers into the labor force is itself a positive achievement which improves income distribution. Accordingly we must modify the analysis to consider trade-offs between national income for the two years rather than merely consumption.

Figure 5–4 shows the relevant diagrammatic analysis. The horizontal axis is consumption today (C_0); the vertical, national income next year (Y_1). The economy can cut back on today's consumption, devoting more resources to investment goods production, which will allow attainment of higher national income levels next year. It is important to note that this year's national income will not itself change; only the consumption-investment mix will. Equilibrium is determined by the tangency of this frontier and the social indifference curve I.

4. After all that, we have still not determined the numerical value of *d*. But from the kit of abstractions we have put together, a final quantification can be gleaned. We do not know, of course, the community's indifference hypersurface for all the years the project will operate. We do not even know it

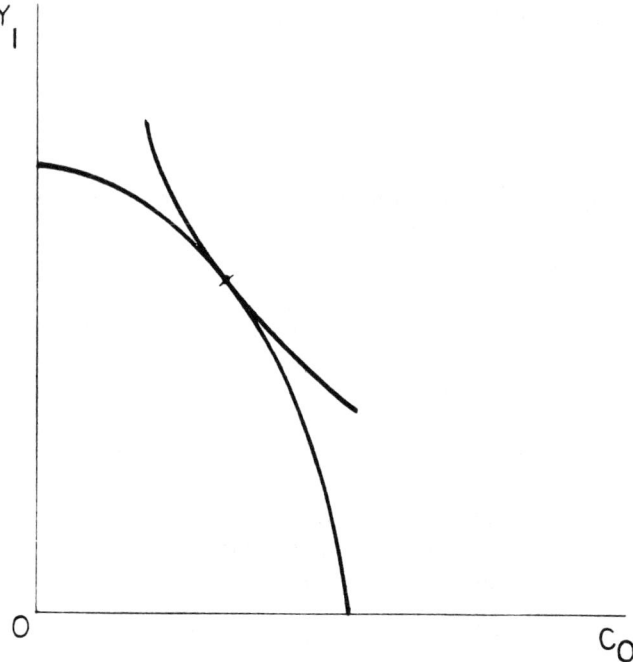

Figure 5–4. Two Period Consumption National Income Frontier

for two years, because the notion of a community indifference curve is itself elusive. Likewise, the transformation curves are unknown, and their dynamics over time can only be guessed at. But all the considerations taken together do tell us what real world concept we can—nearly—isolate and analyze to serve as a surrogate for the social rate of discount, which simultaneously equates the marginal productivity of capital and marginal rate of substitution (or social rate of time preference). In a fully employed economy this is the "real" rate of return on relatively riskless investments. (Although, as our problems show, even this is not a wholly satisfactory approach (Problem 5.3).) This would be the real rate of interest paid on government bonds or super-safe corporate bonds, such as Moody's triple A, around 2–3 percent historically. This is, accordingly, the value we recommend for *d in a noninflationary setting* and for those projects which can legitimately be compared on a common basis. But increasingly we *must* contend with inflation, and caution must be exercised, not only in the selection of a value for *d*, but also in the entire analysis of cost and benefit values. The types of modification necessary are discussed in chapter 10. We must also continue to distinguish insistently those projects which cannot be reduced to a common denominator and allow for them a different criterion—for example, an efficient-budget constraint as in road building, or recovery of investment expenditure through a public sector authority or SOE.

One further caution is required. In any year the total amount of resources centrally budgeted for investment *a priori* may be too little to permit all the projects with a positive net present value to be undertaken. In this case projects should be ranked according to their *relative* NPV, and those with the highest rank undertaken until the allocated investment funds are exhausted (Problem 5.4). But clearly if this goes on for more than a few years, an inefficiency is implied, since apparently worthwhile projects are being neglected. The meaning is clear: society is budgeting too little to be consistent with the adopted rate of discount. Society is giving contradictory messages: it is saying, on the one hand, that it sets a high value on future returns (discounting them so low), yet it is unwilling to sacrifice current income commensurately. Then, either the present share of investment *is* correct and society must recognize this by discounting future income at a higher rate than the 2–3 percent adopted at first, or society's high valuation of future income is correct and it must sacrifice more today. In either event total investment allocations will move closer to total investment requirements.

If foreign borrowings must be resorted to and the country must pay a higher rate because of its tenuous creditworthiness, the discount factor must be raised. This means we have understated the discount factor: while 2–3 percent may be appropriate as the real marginal productivity for advanced industrial economies, it may be too low for developing economies, in which case the international lending rate must be used. Introduction of inflationary impacts on interest rates will be taken up in chapter 10.

The Internal Rate of Return

The IRR is defined as the lowest $\rho_i > 0$ such that for project i,

$$\sum_{i=0}^{T_i} R_{it}(1 + \rho_i)^{-t} = 0.$$

Call this $\bar{\rho}_i$.

R_{it} is the net return in year t (Problems 5.5 and 5.6). This criterion was first espoused because it provides a project ranking which is independent of the rate of interest. This need was recognized, even for private firms, since interest rates could not be known with certainty: since the firm's borrowing rate frequently changes, the set of optimal projects ranked by NPV today might not be the set of optimal projects tomorrow (Problem 5.7). According to the IRR rule, the firm will undertake any project with IRR greater than the interest rate that it must pay, and it will yield a positive return.

At the national economy level the IRR has analogous advantages. Since people disagree on the values to ascribe to the notions of social rate of discount, marginal rate of capital productivity, and social rate of time preference, as well as on which concept to use (so runs the argument), the set of projects which are optimal according to the NPV will depend on the person asked. And, really, who knows what the correct number is? But ranking by IRR is independent of the rate of discount; hence, all that is necessary is to go down the list of projects ranked by IRR until the investable resources allocated for the year are exhausted. But, in general, it is not clear how to determine this total. Some types of exception are network activities, which are discussed below.

Several objections to IRR have been voiced. To understand the most serious of these, we must recall the second motivation for the discounting procedure. The discount coefficient is the rate at which returns could be reinvested to yield further benefits, and the NPV rule ensures that no project will be undertaken unless it yields net benefits at least equal to those of an investment growing at $d(100)$ percent per year. Discounting at $\bar{\rho}_i$, which is what the IRR does, implies that project i will generate net benefits over the years which can be reinvested at that rate until the end of the project life.

There are two difficulties here. First, many of the social benefits are, by their nature, nonreinvestable because they do not constitute ordinary consumption commodities which could, in principle, be considered for reinvestment: a benefit may involve time saving, for example, rather than energy resource production such as coal. However, the same problem exists when using NPV, and we saw how to incorporate this feature into the analysis by adding vertical and horizontal segments into the production frontiers, although this does not completely cope with the essential theoretic problem for NPV or IRR. Second, even if the social benefit does take the form of investable output, for example, coal or consumption goods which might be exported, rather than domestic services, there is no guarantee that the future benefits can be reinvested at $\bar{\rho}_i$. How can this objection be answered?

Now, any project with IRR exceeding d will also pass muster by NPV at a discount rate of d (Problem 5.8), although the rankings of the projects by NPV and IRR will undoubtedly be different (Problem 5.9). This means that if we invest, not in all projects with IRR at least equal to d, but in projects in order of decreasing $\bar{\rho}_i$ until the budget is exhausted, we may invest in some wrong projects. This is certainly true. But recall that we are considering use of the IRR in the first place because we do not know what d really is (Problems 5.10 and 5.11). But if we use a mistaken value for d, we *also* get an incorrect ranking and make wrong decisions. Thus if inadequate knowledge of d is a sufficient reason for objecting to IRR, it is certainly enough reason to object to NPV also. If we do know d, the question of which measure to use need never arise.

The foregoing considerations suggest that the area of application of IRR is in sectors or activities where investment is to be constrained by an efficient budget generated through user revenues—such as road networks. Here the benefits each year will be of a fairly homogeneous kind, although not directly comparable with those in other public sectors. As the highway network expands, links will continue to appear which promise benefits similar to those under review today. The IRR facilitates planning by permitting the establishment of priorities which can be updated yearly. The intranetwork loan financing theory, with investment budget determined by user charges, and shifted around the network, provides the basis for determining the cutoff each year. A situation may prevail in which the IRR of the cutoff project is significantly higher than the rate of discount used elsewhere in the economy. Such a situation, if it persists, suggests that the budget may not be big enough, and user charges should be reviewed and probably increased. Note also that if this excess demand for investment funds prevails when using the IRR, it will probably also occur if NPV is used.

Other objections to the IRR relate to the possibility of multiple roots, negative roots only, or even imaginary roots only (Problem 5.12). According to Descartes' rule, there may be as many different positive roots as there are changes of sign in the R_{it} stream. With $T_i + 1$ time periods there are T_i possible roots. However, few projects or none would have more than two sign changes—one when the project goes on stream and one in the final year of operation when takedown costs, including restoration, may exceed gross benefits. For those with positive and negative signs, clearly the lowest positive root is the relevant one.

Financial Analysis versus Economic Analysis

The contrast is frequently drawn between financial and economic analyses. The first employs market relations and looks at the firm's own costs and benefits (profit). The second attempts to measure benefits and costs from a wider social point of view, and it applies shadow value corrections to individual outputs and inputs when appropriate. Although the IRR and NPV may be used with either approach, some writers use "internal rate of return" to refer only to financial analysis and "economic rate of return" to refer to the analogous calculation based on economic analysis. This usage is ambiguous since it obscures the fact that the essence of both calculations is to determine the rate which equates the discounted benefit stream, however calculated, to the discounted costs.

The main points of contrast between the two types of analysis follow:

1. Depreciation is usually based on historic acquisition cost in financial analysis but on replacement value in economic analysis (provided that the facility would be replaced upon wearing out, which could require that demand be strong enough to cover depreciation of a new facility as well as the currently acquired inputs, including labor).
2. Tariffs and foreign exchange subsidies or penalties are included at face value in financial analysis, but are adjusted, when appropriate, in economic analysis. We reemphasize the need for a careful analysis of the tariff structure to determine whether tariffs should be construed as costs.
3. Labor is shadow priced for economic, but not financial, analysis.
4. Taxes, both direct and indirect, are treated as costs in financial analysis, while in economic analysis they are regarded as transfers, subject to the qualifications discussed in chapter 4—for example, indirect taxes which should be construed as highway user charges. Hence, in economic analysis neither taxes on profits nor indirect taxes are subtracted from gross benefits to reach net benefits.

With such different perspectives it may well happen that an undertaking is viable economically but not financially. In this case economists would argue that the economic criterion should take precedence. In projects which have a large single investment and, subsequent low nondepreciation operating costs (for example, coal, rather than rail car deterioration), the fate of the undertaking depends almost entirely upon the initial decisions; in these there is no question that the economic approach should prevail, as long as the principles employed for shadow valuations are correct, initially, enough technological variants are explored, the economic life can be reasonably thought to be correctly estimated, and so forth. This is the situation of large agricultural amelioration projects, shoreline restoration, navigable waterways, and similar activities.

Projects that are more clearly industrial in nature, or, more generally, projects whose initial investment cost is not as large in relation to subsequent nondepreciation operating costs are apt to be organized on a corporate basis as SOEs. We also argue in later chapters that many projects such as bridges and other isolated transport projects ought to be financed on a corporate basis through revenue bonds redeemed and supported by user charges, because the benefits are virtually impossible to compare with those of other types of activity. In essence we let the market determine the value of a project by letting the bond-buying public estimate the willingness of the potential customers to pay the costs. For these, annual operations will require many additional inputs, and it will be necessary to exercise surveillance over their costs. If their operations are evaluated in economic, rather than financial, terms, they must justifiably operate at a loss. A problem arises, however, because, while losses may be justified on economic grounds, the enterprise may begin to operate sloppily and wastefully, thus generating additional losses which could not be tolerated either on economic or financial grounds. Also, there usually are simply not enough accounting supervisory personnel to examine the necessary operations and ensure that the losses are only those attributable to the initial decision to undertake the project and operate with a loss equal to the difference between the social, shadow-adjusted value of the project and the financial outcome, all calculations based on assumptions of reasonable plant floor efficiency.

If the firm is financed, say, through a state bank loan (or foreign loan) on which interest must be paid, a problem might arise if the discount rate used to calculate NPV is below the rate on the loan, since it might turn out that the project would show up as economically viable yet be unable to repay the loan along the way. We have stressed, however, that discount rates should approximate the rates of interest appropriate for a sector or activity, and if this is done, the danger is obviated somewhat.

Sometimes it may happen that the loan rate is actually sharply lower than the discount rate if the project is financed by a foreign government or supplier. In this instance it will almost certainly happen that the loan is tied to purchases from the lending country and prices are higher to offset the low borrowing cost. In this case the NPV should be figured in relation to the funds that the government itself must put up, with the annual net benefit calculated net of the interest and amortization payments.

Finally, it may be that a project is economically and financially viable, but the financial analysis may uncover a weakness in the project. For example, it may be the case that the loan repayment and cash flow streams diverge. The financial analysis will bring this to light and, if known in advance, a different repayment schedule can be instituted. (Problem 5.13).

Conclusion

The elaboration of the investment criterion is at the heart of public-sector decision making. Measurement of the net social benefit in each year is the subject primarily of the next three chapters; in this chapter we have focused on the way that the benefits in different years should be commensurated. As we have seen, however, matters cannot be treated in complete isolation.

We have argued that the correct concept for commensurating benefits for projects to be compared for central budget allocation is the NPV. This may be absolute or relative, depending on whether or not the investable resources are stipulated in advance. Bear in mind, however, that persistent differences between total investment (implied by choosing all projects with positive

NPV) and the total stipulated yearly by the government budget process imply an inconsistency between society's willingness to postpone consumption, as measured by the chosen rate of discount, and the investment budget. We have also argued that for many activities whose annual budget is currently generated by user charge revenues—a highway network is perhaps the best example to illustrate this approach—an IRR ranking might be used, although an NPV approach where projects are ranked and chosen until investment is exhausted (rather than the strict NPV rule calling for investment whenever NPV is positive) might also be used. We believe that much of the IRR–NPV controversy is of lesser consequence and problems 5.8–5.11 reinforce this view. We believe that the actual approach to the measurement of benefits, not to speak of correct pricing to generate an efficient budget constraint in the first place, and correct estimation of project economic life are usually much more important.

The theory of discounting for the individual is intimately bound up with the concept of the productivity of capital, and we saw that it involved essentially the comparison between what an investment could do in a particular project and its best alternative use. For society the productivity of capital schedule is the important thing—a comparison between potential sacrifice and potential gain on each successively less productive investment project. To determine the precise threshold or equilibrium rate, we must compare the graph showing the consumption possibilities with the graph showing society's preferences, and we must choose that point of investment at which the consumption frontier is tangent to the outermost social consumption indifference curve. The two-period analysis of consumption possibilities was successively generalized to allow for noncommodity consumption, such as time savings value, and other components of national income besides consumption, which is essential for us, because, as we will argue in the following chapters, the national income approach to the measurement of benefits is most appropriate.

But while the social rate of time preference/marginal productivity of capital equality tells us, conceptually, what the discount instrument should be, it provides little in the way of numerical guidance, and the discount rate must be inferred historically by reference to the real rate of return on investments of comparable risk. This does not resolve all problems since there is still room for dispute about what constitutes comparable risk and how to measure inflation. As we have seen, even when settling on some measure as CPI, when it was still unaffected by peculiarities in its calculation, the "real rate" in the United States showed unsettling variability. Some of this is rooted in macro activity levels; some, in inflationary expectations. Its average over a prolonged period, however, was around 2.4 percent. It seems much more reasonable to view this average as a statement of the "true" real rate of interest on riskless investment than simply to take the difference in any year between the prime rate and the CPI change as a measure of that year's true rate with the necessary implication that the true rate and, hence, the MPK can show such extraordinary short-term variation.

As we observed in Problem 5.3, many public-sector investments would be subject to some risk. SOEs comparable to private-sector activities usually make their own investment decisions by responding to interest rates similar to those used by the private-sector firms, so the market itself will force the use of comparable discount rates; analysis of cash flow and loan payback is also instructive. For projects legitimately performed in the public sector which are to be paid for by user charges the willingness to cover costs is itself sign enough of a project's value, reducing the central planner's burden. These projects are not included in the central budget. Then, if discounting at 2–3 percent yields a group of projects with total investment needs appreciably greater than what society deems appropriate and budgets centrally, and this occurs over several years, it is clear that the discount factor is too low. In such cases, however, it is also possible that the net annual benefits are exaggerated, and benefit estimation procedures should also be reviewed.

Problems

5.1. 1. Calculate the net present values of the following revenue time streams at a discount rate of 9 percent and rank the projects.
a. $(-5, 3, 3, 3)$; b. $(-5, 2, 3, 5)$; c. $(-5, 5, 5, -1)$;
d. $(-2.5, 4, 4, -2.5)$; e. $(-2, 1.1, 1.1)$.

2. Which projects would be selected for investment under the NPV rule?

Solution

(1) a. 2.59; b. 3.20; c. 3.03; d. 1.61; e. −.06. Ranking: b,c,d,a,e.

(2) a,b,c and d would be selected since, for them, NPV > 0.

5.2. We first showed that the private firm would undertake any project with NPV > 0. Now, it is often argued that many desirable public sector projects have positive NPV only at lower discount rates. It is often argued that the public sector, whether it gets the funds by borrowing or by taxation, should discount at lower rates than the private sector. (For the moment interest rates are real, rather than nominal, rates determined by supply and demand of real resources. In Problem 5.3 we consider possible deviations between real and nominal rates.) There are at least three justifications for this view:

80 • *Project Decision Making in the Public Sector*

1. The return on public sector investment is believed to be higher than the private return would be from the same projects, possibly because of the high cost of trying to recapture as profits some of the benefits that definitely are there.
2. The public-sector project is typically a very large undertaking involving a great change in consumption, vitiating the idea of a smooth product substitution or consumption frontier. The interest rate appropriate to the last dollar of private-sector investment just before this project is very different from that at the first dollar of the next best investment after this project. Accordingly, the discount rate for these investment dollars on average will be lower than the rate appropriate for the last private investment.
3. The curve shown in figure 5–1 shows *actual* results of the year's investments: some, extremely successful, other, much less so. In anticipation, on the other hand, there would have been very little difference in expected returns for all private projects—after all, nobody would simultaneously invest in projects that he knows are to provide very different returns. It follows then that the *anticipated* product substitution or consumption frontier is much less curved than in figure 5–1. Thus, when we see private projects with high returns we should recall that there are also many with low returns. We should not think of the public-sector discount rate as being much lower than the private rate on the high-return investments, but we should instead think of all returns as being, in anticipation, of about the same order of magnitude as the public-sector investment.

Critically illustrate these ideas within the context of a large water provision project.

Solution

1. This argument is defective as a justification for a lower discount rate. We should ensure that the gains correctly discounted are positive. This proposed approach suggests that a second wrong (incorrect discount rate) be introduced to compensate for the first wrong (inability to calculate benefits). The correct answer is of course to try to correctly measure the benefits. This is difficult. But to say that we have mismeasured them in the first place suggests that the proponent has some idea of the values of the benefits of the services and of water.

2. This argument may be justified for very large public sector investments such as this water project.

3. The actual and expected product substitution curves are shown in figure 5P–1. In terms of expectations, the water project may have a

Comparing Benefits over Time • 81

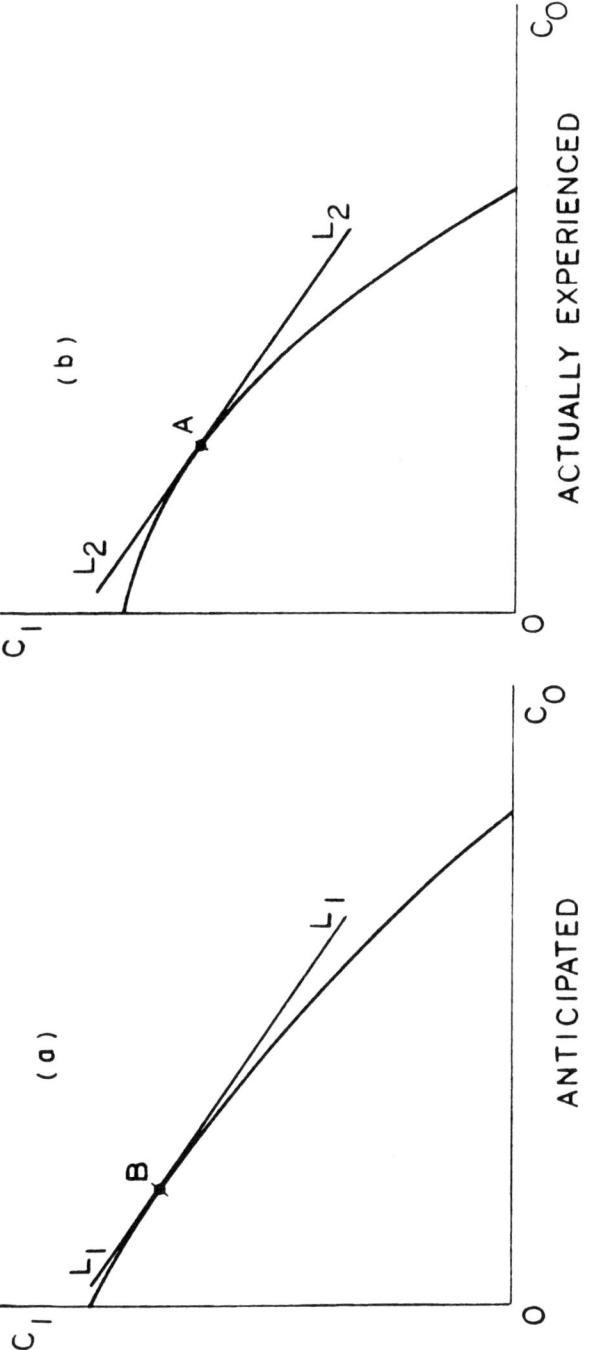

Figure 5P-1. Two Period Consumption Trade off

somewhat smaller return—MPK given by the slope of the tangency at B—than all the private-sector projects, but they are all reasonably close. After the fact, it turns out that the water project return is further to the right at A (although slope L_1 = slope L_2). Note: Using a two-period analysis for this water project is somewhat fanciful, but it conveys the essence of the problem.

5.3. The "real rate of interest" is often defined as the market rate minus the rate of inflation. As reported by the U.S. Department of Commerce, the prime rate in the United States over a prolonged period and the U.S. CPI are shown in table 5P–1. Can the "real rate" as so defined be a reasonable surrogate for the marginal productivity of capital?

Table 5P–1.
Prime Rate, Inflation Rate, and Unemployment Rate

Year	Prime Rate (%)	Change CPI[b] (%)	Unemployment Rate (%)[a]	Real Rate (Prime − CPI Change)
1952	3.0	5.9	3.2	−2.9
1953	3.0	0.9	2.2	2.1
1954	3.3	0.6	4.5	2.7
1955	3.0	−0.5	5.0	3.5
1956	3.5	0.4	4.2	3.1
1957	4.0	2.9	4.2	1.1
1958	4.5	3.0	5.2	1.5
1959	4.0	1.8	6.2	2.2
1960	5.0	1.5	5.7	3.5
1961	4.5	1.5	6.2	3.0
1962	4.5	0.7	6.0	3.8
1963	4.5	1.2	5.4	3.3
1964	4.5	1.6	5.5	2.9
1965	4.5	1.2	4.8	2.3
1966	4.9	1.9	3.9	3.0
1967	6.0	3.4	3.7	2.6
1968	6.0	3.0	3.8	3.0
1969	6.9	4.7	3.4	2.2
1970	8.5	6.1	3.5	2.4
1971	7.0	5.5	6.0	1.5
1972	5.0	3.4	5.9	1.6
1973	5.9	3.4	5.0	2.5
1974	9.8	8.8	5.2	1.0
1975	9.5	12.0	8.2	−2.5
1976	6.8	7.0	7.8	1.8
1977	6.2	4.8	7.3	1.4
1978	8.0	6.8	6.3	1.2
1979	11.8	9.0	5.8	2.8
1980	15.2	13.4	6.2	1.8
1981	19.8	3.8	7.4	16.0

Sources: U.S. Department of Commerce, U.S. Bureau of Labor Statistics.
[a]January of year.
[b]December immediately preceding over December.

Solution

The average real rate over the thirty-year period is 2.4 percent, but between years there is wide variation, ranging from a high of 16.0 percent to a low of −2.9 percent, a difference of 18.9 percentage points. Omitting the last extreme observation yields a range of 6.7 percentage points of variation, still high, and an average of 1.9 percent. Since, moreover, the successive annual differences bounce around so much (there are eighteen changes of sign in the first difference series), the "real rate" so defined cannot be presumed to reflect the marginal productivity of capital in all years, since we would not expect the structure of the economy to change so radically unless the amount of investment changed so sharply from year to year so that the observations would be construed as tangencies at different points on a very curved consumption frontier. This has not been the case. It seems most reasonable, therefore, to take the average of these annual rates. The level of employment is one obvious source of difference in the "real rate" in successive years, but it cannot account for very much of the deviation from constancy.

However, it remains to ask whether this real rate on virtually riskless loans is the magnitude which corresponds to the discount concept. Support for this view is the fact that it is the state which will do the borrowing, and this is what the state must actually pay. However, while these bonds are riskless from the private investor's viewpoint, because the state can always borrow or tax to repay, the outcome of the individual investment may not be so certain. It may be subject to some of the same risk as private sector investments, and so should be discounted by comparable magnitudes. SOEs, whose activity is comparable to activities in the private sector and which, generally speaking, should follow similar behavioral rules (for marketing, investment, and production), will make investments on the basis of interest rates for private firms of similar makeup. For example, a state-owned airline or chemical plant should make calculations on the basis of rates charged to comparable private sector firms (in fact, it should use similar profit criteria in the first place).

5.4. The NPVs for four independent projects for a private firm are calculated as follows, and the investment costs are as shown ($000s). But while the projects are independent in terms of their technologies and markets, the lender for various reasons, does not want to lend to this firm according to the NPV rule for fear of putting too much in one basket, and he restricts himself to $8,000. Check to see that proceeding by the NPV rule is suboptimal for the firm when such capital rationing take place. How might the rule be adjusted to optimize subject to the borrowing constraint. (Assume that the firm cannot find any other lender.)

84 • Project Decision Making in the Public Sector

Table 5P-2
Analysis of NPV under Capital Rationing

Project	$NPV = \sum_{t=0}^{T_i} R_{it}$	$C_0 = I$	Rank
1	12	5.0	2
2	18	8.0	1
3	6	1.8	3
4	3	1.2	4

Solution

If we use absolute (A) NPV we choose project 2 with an ANPV of 18. $C_{02} = 8 =$ borrowing limit. But with rationing we look at Relative (R) NPV. For each project this will be $\sum_{t=1}^{T_i} R_{it}(1 + d)^{-t}/I_i$. This reqires us to add C_0 back to each NPV in column 2 (that is, not deduct it in the first place), giving 17, 26, 7.8, 4.2. The RNPVs are then $17/5 = 3.4$, $26.8 = 3.25$, $7.8/1.8 = 4.2/1.2 = 3.5$. The ranking is now 3,4,1, and 2. Projects 1,3, and 4 with total investment of $8,000 will now be chosen and will yield a total ANPV of 21 versus 18 for 2 alone.

5.5. 1. Recalculate NPV for the projects of Problem 5.1 for discount rates of .02 and .2 and rank them and show that the project rankings depend very heavily on the discount rate used.

2. The internal rate of return furnishes a ranking which is independent of discount rates. For any project it is the smallest positive root of $\sum_{t=0}^{T_i} R_{it}(1 + \rho)^{-t} = 0$, where R_{it} is the net return in year t for the ith project, which has a life of T_i years. Find the IRR for the following time streams:

a. $(-1, 4, -4)$; b. $(-2, 3, -1)$; c. $(-1, 4, -3)$; d. $(-1, 6, -6)$.

Solution

1. Ranking $(d = .02)$: b (4.55); c (3.76); a (3.65); d (2.90); e (.14).
    Note that at this low discount rate, e is also selected.
    Ranking $(d = .2)$: d (2.16); c (2.06); b (1.64); a (1.32); e $(-.32)$.
    All three NPV rankings are different.
2. a. 1, b. 0, c. 2, d. .27.

5.6. For simplicity we used three-period time streams to illustrate the IRR. For the more realistic multiperiod situation, calculations become more trying, n periods involving an $(n - 1)$th degree polynomial equation which has no known easy solution. Solutions are possible by approximating procedures and computer programs exist for them. Write out the polynomial IRR equation for a six-period investment project.

Solution

$R_0 + R_1(1 + \rho)^{-1} + R_2(1 + \rho)^{-2} + R_3(1 + \rho)^{-3} +$
$R_4(1 + \rho)^{-4} + R_5(1 + \rho)^{-5} = 0,$

or

$R_0(1 + \rho)^5 + R_1(1 + \rho)^4 + R_2(1 + \rho)^3 + R_3(1 + \rho)^2 +$
$R_4(1 + \rho)^1 + R_5 = 0.$

5.7. Calculate the NPV of the streams $(-5, 3, 3, 3)$ and $(-5, 2, 3, 4.2)$ at rates of 4 percent and 15 percent. Which project is better?

Solution

	Discount Rate	$D = 4\%$	$d = 5\%$
Project a	$(-5, 3, 3, 3)$	3.32	<u>1.85</u>
Probject b	$(-5, 2, 3, 4.2)$	<u>3.44</u>	1.77

The project which is better at each rate is underlined. Note the switch.

It is interesting to note the conditions under which switches could occur. First it is obvious that if $I_i = I_j$, $T_i = T_j$, and each return stream is constant, one project will have a higher IRR, and it will have a higher NPV at all positive discount rates. Next, if project i has a higher IRR and lower investment cost and return streams are constant, it will be preferred to project j at all positive discount rates. But when a project has higher IRR and higher investment cost, or if the return streams are not constant, the project with the higher IRR will not be preferred to the other at all discount rates.

5.8. Suppose that for all projects there is a negative flow in year zero (the investment) and a positive flow thereafter. Show that, provided there is no rationing of capital, the same projects will be chosen by both the IRR and NPV rules.

Solution

The unrestricted IRR rule is to invest in any project whose IRR $> d$, the rate of discount here taken as the rate of interest. For such a project

86 • Project Decision Making in the Public Sector

$$\sum_{t=0}^{T_i} R_{it}(1 + \bar{\rho}_i)^{-t}, = 0,$$

but for any such i,

$$\sum_{t=0}^{T_i} R_{it}(1 + d)^{-t}, > 0.$$

However, this project would be undertaken by the NPV criterion. Therefore all the same projects will be chosen.

5.9. What can be said if there is capital rationing?

Solution

A different set of projects will probably be chosen by each criterion since there is no guarantee that the rankings are precisely the same.

5.10. A more substantial objection to the IRR is that if the cutoff for IRR-ranked projects is wrong, we will get suboptimal choices. While Problem 5.8 showed that the same projects would be undertaken according to IRR and NPV in the absence of capital rationing, Problem 5.9 explained that, since IRR and NPV rankings were different, if capital is rationed and projects are chosen to exhaust the total investment allocation, different groups of projects could be undertaken. Therefore if a 3 percent cutoff is used in the belief that it is the correct discount rate, and we really should be using 6 percent, the IRR will be wrong and will cause the wrong projects to be chosen. Is this a convincing objection?

Solution

The NPV criterion will also give the wrong ranking, as is evident from the switch in ranking in 5.7. Therefore this is not a convincing objection.

5.11. The objection in 5.10 may be more appropriate for choices between technological variants for a given activity. Suppose variants a and b have the following benefit time streams: a. ($-2.4, 1.7, 1.7$); b. ($-3.0, 1.6, 2.5$). The crossover rate is defined as the discount rate at which the discounted present values of the two streams are equal. Calculate the IRR for a and b, determine the crossover rate, and show that if the discount rate that should be used exceeds the crossover rate, the IRR gives the wrong result.

Solution

$IRR_a = .267$ and $IRR_b = .185$. They are graphed in figure 5P-2.

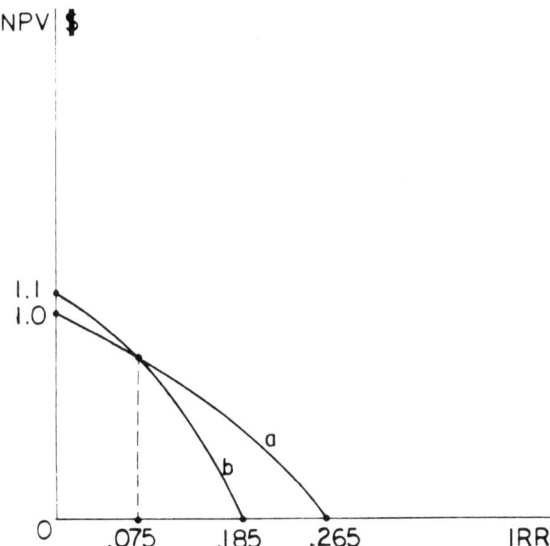

Figure 5P-2. Comparison of NPV and IRR

To determine crossover rate we find the point at which $NPV_a(\rho) = NPV_b(\rho)$, that is, we solve

$$-2.4 + 1.7(1 + \rho)^{-1} + 1.7(1 + \rho)^{-2} = -3.0 + 1.6(1 + \rho)^{-1} + 2.5(1 + \rho)^{-2}.$$

Rewriting we have

$$(-2.4 + 3) + (1.7 - 1.6)(1 + \rho)^{-1} + (1.7 - 2.5)(1 + \rho)^{-2} = 0,$$

or

88 • *Project Decision Making in the Public Sector*

$$.6(1 + \rho)^{-2} + .1(1 + \rho) - .1 = 0$$

and

$$.6\rho^2 + 1.3\rho - .1 = 0,$$

whence $\rho = .075$. (Here $NPV_a = NPV_b = .65$).

If the discount rate that should be used is less than .075, project b is superior (has a higher NPV), but since project a has a higher IRR, it will be chosen, thus giving the wrong result. If the rate that should be used exceeds .075, project a is the correct choice by both IRR and NPV rules. Note that for there to be a crossover rate in the positive quadrant, the project with the greater IRR must have a lower total positive net benefit stream discounted at zero. This requires either that at least one project have an uneven benefit stream or that they have different lives.

5.12. Some writers have objected to the IRR for any or all of the following reasons:
1. There may be multiple roots of the basic equation with more than one greater than zero (for example, Problem 5.5, project d);
2. There may be no positive roots (for example, project b);
3. There may no real roots—all of them may be imaginary.
Show that the sequence $(-3, 5, -3)$ yields no real root. Do you think these objections are critical?

Solution

First we show that the sequence $(-3, 5, -3)$ has no real root. The basic IRR reduces to $-3\rho^2 - \rho - 1 = 0$, with discriminant $\sqrt{1 - 12} = \sqrt{-11} = 3.32i$. Therefore, the two solutions of the equation are imaginary.

We now consider the multiplicity and nonpositiveness of roots. If the lowest positive value of ρ equating $\Sigma_{t=0}^{T_i} R_{it}(1 + \rho)^{-t}$ to zero exceeds the rate proposed as the discount coefficient, the NPV of the project will be greater than zero. To say that there are other values of ρ which equate the sum of discounted benefits to zero is no more significant than saying that there are many discount rates which permit an NPV of any project to exceed zero.

Moreover, the number of positive roots cannot exceed the number of changes of sign in the benefit stream. However, normally we would expect at most two sign changes—when we move from investment stage to full operation at the start, and when we have closedown costs at the end (for example, environmental restoration).

The type of project stream necessary for imaginary roots is curious, with negative returns even at a zero discount rate. It is difficult to imagine any such projects seriously or knowingly being considered.

5.13. It is proposed to build a new cement plant in Ecalpon with financing by means of supplier credits from a foreign country. Because it is such a large project and there is a shortage of technically trained managerial staff in the country, it is believed that the plant can be better managed by the public sector, so it is decided to establish an SOE for the purpose. The capital cost will be $50,000,000 at 10 percent. It is initially proposed to repay it in constant blended annual payments over an eight-year term. There are no labor market or fiscal distortions. The gross revenue and other important measures (in millions of dollars) are shown in table 5P–4. (The loan repayment calculations assume that payments are made monthly, the figures given being the annual totals.) The rise in costs in the ninth year is due to increased maintenance needs for the aging capital equipment.

Financial analysis may be conducted in terms of cash flow or net profit, the essential difference between them being the deduction of depreciation to calculate the net profit. (Of course, depreciation does affect cash flow calculations to the extent that it bears on taxes to be paid.) No matter, the project is almost certainly desirable from a national viewpoint since (1) the taxes would not be considered a social cost, and (2) the equipment will have a twenty-year economic life, so it will generate benefits far beyond the ten-year period over which it is decided to depreciate it. However, whether profit or cash flow is relied upon, the measured benefits will be negative for the first eight years while the loan is being repaid: this is shown by the cash flow net of interest and principal in column 13 and by subtracting the principal repayment from the profit in column 8.

The financial analysis can never be dispensed with, since it tells us the evolving need for foreign exchange and also shows the amount of support that the project will require in the form of temporary subsidies as long as net cash flow is negative. While the project will still be desirable, the particular stream of payments may present problems which can only be exposed by financial analysis. Moreover, the firm's operations will subsequently be evaluated in terms of profits. This is more difficult if there are sharp swings in the annual profit stream, as is the case here, since in any particular year expected profits or losses may be confounded with losses due to sloppy internal cost control, thus undermining managerial accountability. For example, the plant may fail to repair its electrostatic air filter in the chimney, allowing 7 percent of its production to go with the wind. Show how the repay-

Table 5P-3
Financial Analysis of Ecalpon Cement Corp.

Year	(1) Gross Revenue	(2) Nondepreciation Costs	(3) Gross Profits before Depreciation	(4) Depreciation	(5) Blended Annual Payment Interest	(6) Blended Annual Payment Principle	(7) Blended Annual Payment Total	(8) Net Profit before Tax (3)−(4)−(5)	(9) Tax (40%)	(10) Net Profit after Tax (8)−(9)	(11) Gross Cash Flow (10)−(14)+(15)	(12) Cash Flow Less Interest (11)−(5)	(13) Cash Flow Less (Interest+Principle) (12)−(6)
1	11	4.5	6.5	5	4.6	4.4	9.0	−3.1	0	−3.1	6.5	1.9	−2.5
2	11	4.5	6.5	5	4.2	4.8	9.0	−2.7	0	−2.7	6.5	2.3	−2.5
3	13	4.5	6.5	5	3.7	5.3	9.0	−0.2	0	−0.2	8.5	4.8	−0.5
4	13	4.5	8.5	5	3.2	5.8	9.0	0.3	0.1	0.2	8.4	5.2	−0.6
5	13	4.5	8.5	5	2.6	6.4	9.0	0.9	0.4	0.5	8.1	5.5	−0.9
6	13	4.5	8.5	5	2.0	7.0	9.0	1.5	0.6	0.9	7.9	5.9	−1.1
7	13	4.5	8.5	5	1.2	7.8	9.0	2.3	0.8	1.5	7.7	6.5	−1.3
8	13	4.5	8.5	5	0.5	8.5	9.0	3.0	1.2	1.8	7.3	6.8	−1.7
9	13	5.5	7.5	5	0.0	0.0	0.0	2.5	1.0	1.5	6.5	6.5	6.5
10	13	5.5	7.5	5	0.0	0.0	0.0	2.5	1.0	1.5	6.5	6.5	6.5
11	13	5.5	7.5	0	0.0	0.0	0.0	7.5	3.0	4.5	4.5	4.5	4.5
12	13	5.5	7.5	0	0.0	0.0	0.0	7.5	3.0	4.5	4.5	4.5	4.5
13	13	5.5	7.5	0	0.0	0.0	0.0	7.5	3.0	4.5	4.5	4.5	4.5
14	13	5.5	7.5	0	0.0	0.0	0.0	7.5	3.0	4.5	4.5	4.5	4.5
15	13	5.5	7.5	0	0.0	0.0	0.0	7.5	3.0	4.5	4.5	4.5	4.5

ment schedule can easily be adjusted to eliminate the financial losses in any year.

Solution

These problems will be reduced if financial analysis inputs are completely harmonized with economic analysis inputs. This would mean here that we employ a longer depreciation schedule and urge the foreign lender to lend for a longer period to reduce the annual principal repayment needs. For example, if the lender were willing to lend for the full twenty years of the expected equipment life, the annual blended payment would fall by 37 percent from $8.96 million to $5.62 million). Note, however, that the project is given no special consideration by virtue of its public-sector subordination.

Bibliographic Note

The basic diagramatic two-period analysis originated with Irving Fisher. This analysis refers to individuals or firms. Extension to the economy, and consideration of various problems involved therein to derive a single discount rate, has been undertaken by a number of writers, including Feldstein, Sen, Marglin, and Harberger (in Layard), cited in chapter 1. These papers attempt to make concrete notions such as marginal productivity and opportunity cost of capital, social rate of time preference, and social rate of discount. On a different plane are a number of papers collected by Ezra Solomon in *The Management of Corporate Capital* (New York: The Free Press, 1959). Papers by Hirshleifer, Lorie and Savage, and Alchian concerning paradoxes in the internal rate of return stimulated much of the thinking presented in this chapter. They are generally critical of the IRR, but their criticism is almost entirely in terms of contrast to a knowable, correct, and constant rate of interest to serve as the discount coefficient.

6
Principles of Benefit Measurement

We turn to the measurement of the net annual benefit R_{it}. One of the most commonly used approaches to the evaluation of benefits—consumer surplus (problem 6.1)—requires, for correct application, very special conditions which are apt to be honored most often in the breach. Extended discussion of this concept is reserved until chapter 9. The present chapter takes up the wide range of criteria which we refer to as "rectangular," and in the next two chapters specific applications are made in secularly fully employed and not fully employed economies.

The National Income Approach

Why should there be any disagreement about the way benefits are measured in the first place? Ideally, we would like to measure directly the change in "national economic welfare" following an investment. But there is no cardinal measure of welfare. So we ask, "If there were some such measure of welfare, how would it behave?" Of all the measures of performance that we do have, which one could be construed to vary most directly with a cardinal welfare measure, if such a measure existed?

The rectangular criteria that have been used, sometimes only by local interests seeking some investment for their district out of central funds, include concepts as varied as employment increase, local cost reduction, sales flowing from a project, national income change, and others.

As will be apparent through many problems, in chapters 6–8, national income benefit calculations may be extraordinarily difficult, involving as they do a complex web of interactions and interrelated consequences. However, in the secularly fully employed economy, it is possible to use various surrogates, such as cost reduction, since assuming secularly full employment implies that resources economized will be directly taken up into production, thus raising real income and welfare. Profits and changes therein are another useful surrogate; profit may rise because costs are reduced, while, at least at the start, selling prices do not fully reflect these reductions, or because price reductions lead to greater demand for other goods with a net addition to profit. The main implication of all this is that leaving many investment decisions to firms concerned with profit maximization and cost reduction, whether operating in the private or public sectors, is consistent with welfare gains. On the other hand, a measure like total revenue has no relationship to either real income or welfare, since it might increase merely because of organizational change, such as lesser vertical integration.

In the unemployed economy, however, the relationship between cost reduction, or profit, and national income is not known, or else is indeterminate. We explore this issue further in chapter 8. For now, we merely observe that if cost reduction involves layoffs of workers who cannot be immediately reabsorbed into the labor force, it reduces welfare. On the other hand, if the workers do find some alternative employment, cost reduction, real income, and welfare will move together. But in this case we must also calculate the contribution of the released and reemployed workers, so that cost reduction by itself is not enough.

Since advocacy of national income may seem controversial to analysts who have relied on other benefit measurements, such as consumer surplus, and, more generally, to those who have been exposed primarily to the criticisms of the weakness and inadequacy of national income measures as indicators of economic welfare, a few further words in its defense are in order. The traditional criticisms of the welfare significance (or insignificance) of national income measures can be grouped essentially into three classes:

1. paradoxes or quirks of national accounts procedures (problem 6.2);
2. the failure of the accounts to measure externalities;
3. the index number problem (problem 6.3).

The first two criticisms, we conclude, are overly severe. The third is important when measuring benefits over long periods; but apt to be even more important in such cases is the elusiveness of the object of measurement—the near impossibility of pinning down the sequence of events to try to determine the net value-added associated with investments of the type which are usually of greatest concern to public sector bodies—a bridge or a new airport, for example (problem 6.4). These investments entail many complex impact patterns rather than simple production of reasonably homogeneous commodities. In such cases it is necessary to rely on a physical measure, and the challenge is to project allocatively efficient demand or to ensure that physical projections imply a social value which is not less than their social cost. This often requires imposing a financial recovery constraint on the responsible agency.

But it would be a weak defense of the national accounts approach if all that could be said were that traditional objections exaggerate the inability of national income to reflect welfare. On a more positive note, this approach has the following virtues (see problems 6.5–6.9; these may be more instructive following the review of national income calculations in the next section):

1. It gives the microeconomic planner the same type of criterion as the macroeconomic policymaker for whom GNP is the main indicator of national economic performance. This cannot be said of consumer surplus, physical criteria, or other rectangular value measures such as industry sales (problem 6.5).
2. It provides an organizing framework to classify cost and benefits which helps us avoid double counting of two kinds: double counting of vertically nonintegrated processes to calculate value-added (problem 6.6), and double counting of results which are essentially different, such as wages and consumption (problem 6.7). It also provides guidance to know when two elements apparently from opposite sides of the ledger *should* be added together rather than subtracted, as will sometimes be necessary in the unemployed economy (problem 6.8).
3. It provides precedence and guidance, though not always the numbers, necessary for valuing nonmarket effects, for example, imputed rents of owner-occupied buildings or farm-gate price imputations for farm consumption in kind (problem 6.9).
4. In contrast to consumer surplus, it encourages thinking about the intimate connection between user charges and cost relationships.
5. Adequate surrogate measures are available when the national accounts measure cannot be calculated because of the complexity of the projected developments. This is especially true in the fully employed economy.

The Essence of National Income Calculations

The expression "national income" is used in three senses in economics:

1. as a nontechnical expression for the total output of an economy, implicitly assuming that the produced commodities can be added together in a meaningful way; this is usually the sense in economic theory, on the one hand, and in loose discussion about macroeconomic relations, on the other (for example, "a fall in interest rates will stimulate employment and national income");
2. a carefully defined technical expression for a macroeconomic magnitude, namely the income side of the national accounts; when we speak of national income as a definitional term, this is usually what we mean, although the full name for this expression, in Canada, for example, is

"Net National Income at Factor Cost" (Statistics Canada, *National Income and Expenditure Accounts*. Vol. 3. p. 69);

3. the main national macroeconomic aggregate—for example, GNP, GNE, PIB (for example, in Brazil)—all of which are similar in concept and differ from GDP in their treatment of payments and receipts to and from foreign and non-residential factors of production.

In this book, by "national income" we mean the last usage—the methodology underlying the macroeconomic accounts, which in most Western developed, and developing, nations is similar. The essence of this methodology is the attempt to sum up the total productive activity of an economy by a single number or set of numbers. Naturally, we do not conceive of every investment as having nationwide impacts; regional income changes, calculated essentially by the same methodology, may be the measure of interest. As noted above, one of the advantages of this approach is that we often can decentralize investment decision-making through the use of surrogate measures and local agencies. GNP is preferred to GDP because it focuses more emphatically on net benefits when the projects are financed by foreign loans, deducting from the total projected benefit stream the loan repayments as they are made and thus providing a net stream to compare with any investment of domestic funds necessary at the outset. This is, of course, more compatible with private-sector investment requiring foreign capital.

Most readers are familiar with the general outline of the national accounts. It is summarized under major rubric in table 6–1 as a convenience for the following discussion. Especially to be noted is the fact that the owner-occupied house rent imputations would show up both as consumption and as income of nonfarm unincorporated business including rent (problem 6.10). Other consumption and income imputations (for example, on-farm consumption) are added in the relevant line item (problem 6.10).

It is easy to see the effects of changes in various components. Increasing farm production will increase income (in real terms) and consumption. Increases in farm prices without an increase in production will raise nominal income but will not change real income. A decision to increase farm consumption imputations above farm-gate wholesale prices will not change any underlying real relations, but it will raise nominal income; but then applying the new prices to past years' production will show real income unchanged.

Suppose real production costs fall. These ultimately translate into labor input reduction, but, if the economy is a self-adjusting mechanism, that is, the fully employed situation here assumed, the labor will be reabsorbed and create additional output. If profits rise, under constant velocity of money and unchanged money supply, when an industry introduces a technologically superior product, nominal income does not change, but if we adjust the prod-

Table 6–1
Basic Set-Up of National Accounts

Income Side	Expenditure or Product Side
Wages, salaries, and supplementary labor income	Personal expenditure on consumer goods and services
Military pay and allowances	Government current expenditure on goods and services
Corporation profits before taxes	
Deduct: Dividends paid to nonresidents	Gross fixed capital formation Government Business:
Interest and miscellaneous investment income paid to residents	Residential construction Nonresidential construction and machinery and equipment
Accrued net income of farm operators from farm production	
Net income of nonfarm unincorporated business including rent	Value of physical change in inventories: Government Business
Inventory valuation adjustment	
	Exports of goods and services
Net National Income at factor cost	Deduct: Imports of goods and services Residual error of estimate
Net National Income at factor cost	
Indirect taxes less subsidies	
Capital consumption allowances and miscellaneous valuation adjustments	
Residual error of estimate	
Gross National Product at market prices	Gross National Expenditure (or Product) at market prices

uct price for quality change, this year's nominal output is seen to be worth more than last year's.

We remind the reader that full employment is a secular notion; cyclical shortfalls from full employment do not obviate the applicability of this framework for such economies. On the other hand, the whole nation may not be fully employed; pockets of long-term or secular depression may coexist, and these should be treated by the methods of chapter 8. The Appalachia region in the United States represents such an example. Conversely, there may be a virtually fully employed region in developing economies; the São Paulo city region in Brazil, and possibly all of São Paulo state, might be cited here.

The foreign-trade sector requires special mention, especially for underdeveloped economies where there may be a large capacity to expand without diverting resources from other domestic uses. Here, the national income criterion is most easily measured as the difference between export value and total imports. Care must be taken to ensure not only that incremental input costs—for example, rail improvement to reduce bottlenecks—are deducted from export sales, but also that such services are priced correctly to promote rational decisions elsewhere and in the future. If a country's production can influence export prices, the foreign-trade revenue may be harder to estimate before the undertaking, but prices following project implementation are what should be studied and used to measure real income change (problem 6.11).

Thus, the profit-maximizing or cost-reducing behavior of firms is consistent with use of national income to measure benefits in the private sector, provided that the firms are competitive or, if monopolistic, regulation is efficient. This can be said for SOEs in the manufacturing sector as well, again provided that they are efficiently regulated and made to play by the same rules as private firms, which would require, among other things, that access to loans be on an equal footing—no preferential borrowing rates due to implicit or explicit government backing.

Investments by transportation firms and other services, such as the post office, should also be conducted in this way, although here more explicit subsidies for specific services may be required—for example, subsidies to operations in sparse or outlying areas. These should be consistent with the distribution and political/national goals, as envisaged in the theory of public-sector participation and pricing, discussed in chapter 3, but these will usually be operating, rather than investment, expenditures.

It is the area of activities more traditionally performed in the public sector and requiring sizable investment, primarily various forms of infrastructure, that prompts greatest doubts about the existence of a surrogate for national income measurement: if we want to use the national income approach to measure the benefit of an airport, bridge, tunnel, baseball stadium, or convention center, how do we simulate or anticipate the complex set of interrelationships following from the investment and net out all the intermediate flows to reduce everything to a net value-added measure? If we are unable to do this, can a surrogate-like cost reduction or profit be used for the purpose? We turn to this difficult question in the next chapter.

Problems

6.1. Let $q(p) = 7000 - 2.2p$ be the market demand curve for refrigerators, where p is given in dollars, and suppose the price today is $1,250. The traditional (so-called Marshallian) consumer surplus is equal to the area of the triangle between the demand curve and the horizontal line at $1,250. Calculate it. The change in CS associated with a price change is the difference between the area of the corresponding triangle after the change and the first triangle. Calculate the change in CS following a fall in price to $500.

Solution

$q(p) = 7000 - 2.2p,$ $\quad p(q) = 3182 - 4545q,$

$q(0) = 7000,$ $\quad p(0) = 3182,$

$q(1250) = 7000 - 2750 = 4250,$

$q(500) = 7000 - 1100 = 5900,$

$CS(1250) = [(3182 - 1250) \times 1250]/2 = \$4,105,500$ (area A),

$CS(500) = [(3182 - 500) \times 5900]/2 = \$7,911,900$ (area A + area B),

$\Delta CS = \$7,911,900 - 4,105,500 = \$3,806,400$ (area B).

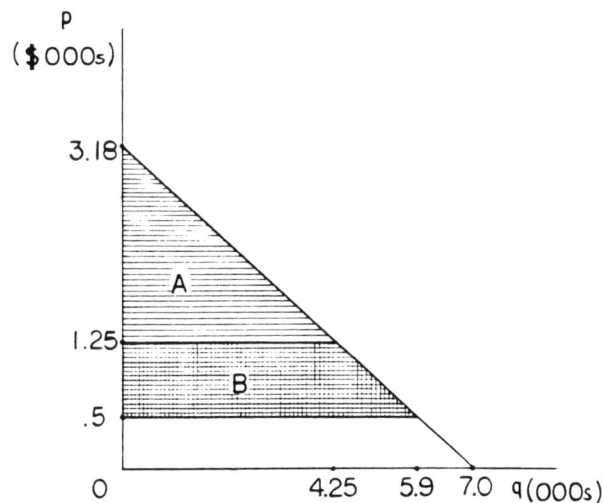

Figure 6P–1. Traditional Consumer Surplus Diagram

The triangle formula is adequate for linear demand functions. For the general situation, however, we must integrate the demand function. Thus, in this case we have

$$CS(1250) = \int_{1250}^{3182} (7000 - 2.2)\,p\,dp = \$4,105,000,$$

$$CS(500) = \int_{500}^{3182} (7000 - 2.2)\,p\,dp = \$7,911,000,$$

$$\Delta CS = \int_{500}^{1250} (7000 - 2.2)\,p\,dp = \$3,806,000.$$

6.2. Examples are the country squire who decides to marry his housekeeper, or the father who pays his son to mow the lawn rather than give him an allowance. In the first example national income falls because this exchange no longer takes place; in the second, it rises as a new transaction arises, but in neither case is there a change in welfare. The criticism is correct, but the problem is not very severe. What of farm consumption in kind, tomatoes at the wholesale price of $2.00 a basket, say, which will be combined with home labor to produce juice, pasta, and so on, which would, of course, have a much higher value if purchased?

Solution

From the national GNP point of view, primary interest resides in the rate of growth. As long as the sector affected is small, the rate of growth (or, indeed, even the level) of GNP will not be seriously affected. Even if the sector is large, if the rate of growth of physical output is comparable to GNP growth, there will be little effect from undervaluing the in-kind consumption. Placing a higher valuation on in-kind farm consumption would require us to revalue earlier output also, and the rate of growth would be unchanged. In any case, the precedent has been established. If some other price is more reasonable, it must be used. This is probably the case for much of the in-kind farm consumption.

6.3. Figure 6P–2 shows indifference curves I_1 and I_2 for two years for an economy with two goods, the quantities of which are denoted x and z. Consumption in the two years takes place at points A and B, where the indifference curves are tangent to the price lines which express total national income, namely $Y_1 = x_1 p_{x1} + z_1 p_{z1}$ and $Y_2 = x_2 p_{x2} + z_2 p_{z2}$. Clearly, the consumption vector of B (year 2) is preferred to that at A, since it is on a higher indifference curve. In general, however, knowing Y_1 and Y_2 only and not knowing the indifference curves will not enable us to rank the situations, since one may be higher than the other simply because of higher prices for one or both commodities. We must compare real national income for the two years, that is, the sum of the quantities produced, weighted by the same prices. However, we may use prices of either year 1 or year 2. That is, we would compare the first equation above (income of year 1 expressed in year 1 prices, denoted Y_{11}) to income of year 2 expressed in year 1 prices, $Y_{21} = x_2 p_{x1} + z_2 p_{z1}$, and the second equation (income of year 2 expressed in year 2 prices, denoted Y_{22}) to $Y_{12} = x_1 p_{x2} - z_1 p_{z2}$, income of year 1 expressed in year 2 prices. In each case we may express z in terms of the other variables, for example, $z_1 = Y_{12}/p_{z2} - x_1 p_{x2}/p_{z2}$. For $x_1 = 0$ the value of z_1 may be called $\hat{Y}_{12}$. This tells us how many units of z may be bought with the income of year 1 expressed in year 2 prices. Other values are read similarly.

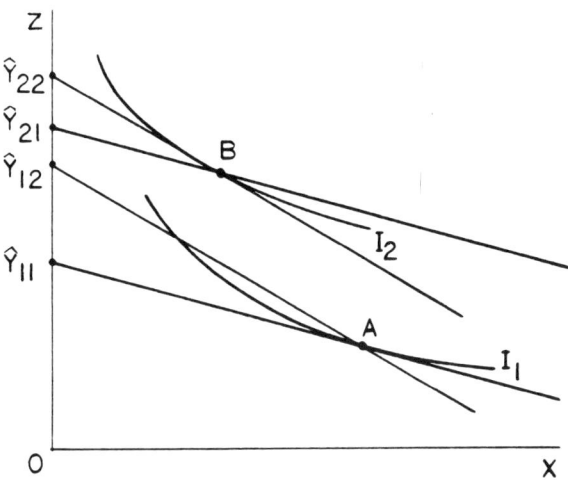

Figure 6P–2. Two Situations with Different Tastes and Consumption Patterns and Consistent National Income Comparisons

Now in figure 6P–2 the output of year 2 is preferred to that of year 1, and both z-equivalent income measures of year 2 are higher than those of year 1, that is, $\hat{Y}_{22} > \hat{Y}_{12}$ and $\hat{Y}_{21} > \hat{Y}_{11}$. However, this need not be the case. The "index number problem," in its most perverse form, occurs precisely because one year's income shows up higher than that of a second in one set of prices, and the ranking is reversed with the other set of prices. Can you draw an indifference curve diagram where this occurs?

Solution

An example is shown in figure 6P–3. This is likely to happen when there are radical shifts in the output and consumption mix.

102 • *Project Decision Making in the Public Sector*

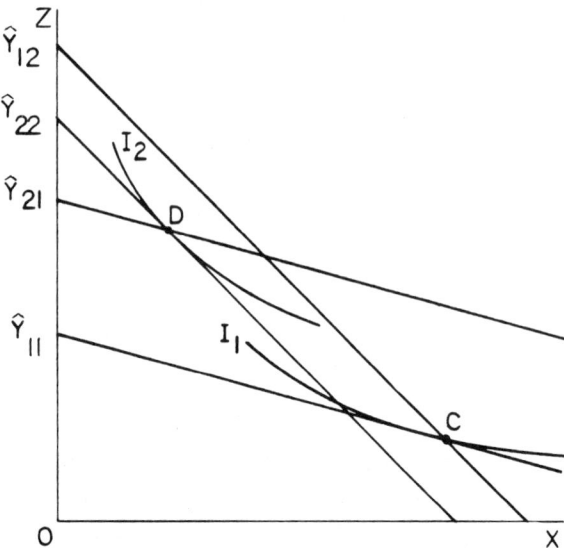

Figure 6P-3. Two Situations with Different Tastes and Consumption Patterns and Conflicting National Income Comparisons

6.4. A new airport is being planned. What will be the annual national income impact (positive, negative, or neutral) of the following related events:

1. 1,000,000 more people will travel each year;
2. some will be tourists with unknown destinations;
3. some will be business people who will rely less on telephone and corporate jets;
4. some will purchase liquor on board;
5. some will purchase magazines, and so on, at newsstands; some will purchase fewer elsewhere;
6. the bus companies will run fewer buses;
7. some people will purchase houses closer to the airport;
8. some houses will be purchased and demolished to be replaced with factories for which airport noise will not be a problem;
9. during construction some workers will be deflected from other tasks and jobs;
10. more life insurance will be sold;
11. some house values elsewhere in the city will fall somewhat; others will rise.

Could CS provide a meaningful alternative?

Principles of Benefit Measurement • 103

Solution

It is not possible to trace through all impacts, value them correctly, and predict their future evolution, all of which is necessary to determine value-added. This is why it is often necessary to rely on a physical output measure, but one which is efficiently generated, that is, in which the prices that are responded to themselves reflect as fully as possible the preferences, tastes, and income constraints of the people as well as the true social costs. In this case this requires that full costs be recovered locally, apart from explicit national policy grants (for example, air defense signals which may require local radio tower time, or sovereignty overflights which may originate at this airport).

Frequently a country will have a policy of imposing airport ticket taxes for international flights and nothing for domestic trips. Partly, this may be justified as an attempt to discriminate through use of the different demand intensities of the domestic and foreign flights. But it is also due, undoubtedly, to a preference for minimizing the domestic political fallout. This necessarily leads to higher levels of domestic flight activity and creates pressures to expand capacity.

It is difficult to see how CS could provide an easily calculable alternative.

6.5. 1. Suppose an agricultural project could yield an annual net GNP change of $100,000 in the form of fruit exports (labor to be used is otherwise unemployed). On the other hand, a 10-kilometer road to connect a new small airport to a summer recreation area yields a zero net national income change and a net annual CS of $120,000. (Never mind for a moment the problems of calculating either.) Both projects require an initial investment of $1,500,000. Under the CS criterion which project would be chosen? (Note: You can decide how to measure CS of the agricultural project from the fact that CS theory requires constancy of the marginal utility of money.) Is there a conflict with the macro level planning which seeks to maximize rate of growth of the national income in the economy?

2. "The city will lose $20,000,000 in annual revenue if this convention hall is not built." Comment.

Solution

1. The GNP and CS of the projects are as shown (annual benefits):

	Airport Project	Agricultural Project
GNP	0	100,000
CS	120,000	100,000[a]

[a]Since MUM is constant, each dollar of export earnings brings just one dollar of utility. See chapter 9.

By CS the airport will be selected. But it is counterproductive from a national income point of view, since we must forgo the agricultural project which would raise GNP, the main macroeconomic performance measure.

2. This is a wholly meaningless statement, since there is no way to know how much double counting there is, that is, what is the net value-added. For example, revenue would increase if hotels contracted out their dining needs, since the hotels would then receive the money in the first place and would pay some to outside chefs, rather than their own. Be especially skeptical of project recommendations based on such claims.

6.6. Suppose from the $100,000 of annual output in 6.5.1, the farms had to subtract expenses for imported fertilizer—$10,000 annually. What would be the effect on net NY?

Solution

The net change would fall by $10,000 to $90,000.

6.7. Suppose the net agricultural output of $100,000 in 6.5.1 is only part of the net benefit. In addition, the following effects are observed:

1. A local basket weaving industry is established which produces annual sales of $5,000. Some baskets are used by farmers to gather crops ($1,000), some are used at home for various purposes ($2,500), and the rest are exported.
2. The local populace begins to consume $3,000 of cooking utensils annually (brought in from a fully employed major industrial city) and $4,000 of mattresses (also brought in).

How will the benefit measure be affected?

Solution

1. The baskets in crop gathering ($1,000) must be subtracted from the total product, since they are an intermediate input necessary for production, but then added in to total income, since the workers have no alternative employment. However, the $2,500 of purchases for other purposes and the exports ($1,500) have not otherwise been considered and must be added, raising the total benefit by $4,000.

2. If the city is operating at capacity, these purchases must be diverted from potential buyers elsewhere so there will be no GNP change. How-

ever, these goods are relatively low technology, and it would be expected that a local supplier using local unemployed labor will soon start up, or that additional workers will move to the city to expand capacity there. In either case it would be reasonable to add these flows to the annual benefit starting a few years hence.

6.8. Suppose all the baskets in 6.7 are consumed locally. We know this through a user survey rather than a producer survey, since the producers are harder to identify. How does this affect the calculation?

Solution

The agricultural output in 6.5.1 is exported from the region, netting $100,000 less $10,000 (fertilizer) or $90,000, which breaks down into profit and wages, principally the latter. In addition, we find that $5,000 worth of baskets are being purchased and used locally, and of this it is determined that $1,000 worth is an intermediate input into fruit production, which we reasoned should be subtracted and then added back in. Thus, $4,000 is being consumed. Now, consumption and wages are opposite sides of the ledger; however, in this case we should add the $90,000 and the $4,000, since the latter does not take away from other production. That is, although the $4,000 worth of baskets are purchased with money coming into the region from the sale of crops, it should be added to the $90,000 to determine the total change in our national income measure: essentially, we are producing $94,000 more worth of final output. It was merely a matter of convenience that the $90,000 was calculated by reference to the financial position of the farmers (which is on the income side of the accounts), rather than by going out and physically counting the crops, while it happened to be more convenient to count the baskets (the expenditure side) rather than the income of the basket weavers.

Also see problems 8.1. and 8.2.

6.9. 1. In a project to clear a river valley of malaria and institute agricultural production, the newcomers will have to build themselves some housing—simple adobe "beehive" type units. In cities not too far distant, housing of comparable quality rents for $8 per month. What guidance does this provide for treatment of housing in the agricultural project?

2. Suppose one reason the new settlers have come here is the continued long-term drought in their place of origin, and they could not get anything for their housing when they left. How does this affect your calculation?

Solution

1. There is an annual rent imputation of $96 for owner-occupied housing. In addition, there is a benefit measured by the initial construction activity. In GNP the house construction represents capital investment, the rent a services flow. (Of course, depreciation must be subtracted to determine Net National Income, as well as Net Annual Benefit). (Also see problem 8.3).

2. The housing will be abandoned. However, no deduction from GNP should be made since the loss of value was unexpected (just as there is no deduction for buildings destroyed by bombs in wartime, in contrast to planned scrapping, the idea being that the former does not reflect badly on the country's productive ability whereas replacement of deteriorated capital implies that economic forces were acting in two directions).

6.10. 1. Suppose that 1,000,000 homeowners in the economy suddenly change their behavior patterns and decide to rent to each other for $500 per month. Assuming no taxes, interest, or insurance, how would GNP be affected if *there were no* owner-occupied imputation? (There was such an incipient tendency in Canada in early 1982 because doing this could enable homeowners to deduct mortgage interest and property taxes as a business expense. In contrast to the United States such expenses are not deductable on personal use property.)

2. Assuming that $500 does adequately reflect the rental value of these houses, show how to treat it in the national accounts table when the houses are lived in by their owners.

Solution

1. It would rise by $12 \times 500 \times 1,000,000$, or $6 billion.

2. In the normal course of affairs, there is an imputation of $6 billion for owner-occupied housing, falling under the rental income rubric, and $6 billion for consumption on the expenditure side of the ledger.

6.11. Chrome is in limited world supply, produced by only a few nations, including several characterized by political instability. Ecalpon today exports some chrome at the world price of $500/ton. A new large deposit in Ecalpon has an excellent outlook, but a major railroad expansion is needed to get the ore to port. But its cost, together with mine development costs, might lead to prices higher than those now existing. In the calculation the miners are to be paid the wage presently common to comparable domestic industries, and it is known that they will not work for less. If the project is undertaken it will be on the basis of long-term contracts with a price escalator clause based on a world inflation index. What rail price policy should be pursued?

Solution

If the potential miners are now unemployed, their employment must be counted a benefit. If the total revenue, less railroad and port costs, nonlabor mine operating costs, and administration, is less than the labor cost, there will be a financial loss unless a subsidy is granted. On the other hand, here the annual benefit would be correctly calculated as the sum of the labor costs and profit, less railroad and port costs, and so on, discounted at the correctly set MPK. If the discounted stream is positive, the project should be undertaken. The subsidy can be given either in the form of a contribution toward the railroad construction or an operating grant. The latter is preferable, since it can be reduced in accord with price escalation in the future. This policy will help enforce managerial discipline in this project and, thence, elsewhere in the economy.

Bibliographic Note

Criticisms of the national accounts as welfare measure, especially the index number problem, are well known. It is worth reemphasizing that index number relativity is most bothersome when long time periods are under study; it is much less consequential over short planning horizons.

National income criteria were not used in some of the earliest and most extensive types of project evaluation—transport projects—partly because the impacts of a general purpose project were so diverse that it was thought easier to concentrate on the output of the activity itself rather than ultimate consequences. The immediate output was traffic. It was thought that reductions in the cost of travel were adequate measures of the ultimate effects, and these would be best reflected by a consumer surplus trapezoid. Problems with consumer surplus are left mainly for chapter 9. An excellent survey of consumer surplus, including an excellent bibliography, is given by Currie, Murphy, and Schmitz. Other consumer surplus references are given following chapter 9.

Instructive examples of national income benefit measurement for transport projects are given by Bergmann, Tinbergen, and Bos and Koyck. Most scholarly papers do not pursue a national income approach for infrastructure projects, however. Nor, typically, do consultants' studies, except when export development is concerned. On the other hand, industrial or agricultural projects generally do calculate benefits following more or less explicitly the national income idea. Clearly, use of consumer surplus in some sectors only will bias investment, all other things equal, toward the sectors which do use it. The books by Gittinger, Lal, and Scott, MacArthur, and Newberry, cited below or in chapter 1, also include many useful case studies and procedures.

References

Bergmann, Barbara. "The Cochabamba-Santa Cruz Highway in Bolivia." In *The Impact of High Investment on Development,* edited by George W. Wilson, Barbara R. Bergmann, Leon V. Hirsch, and Martin S. Klein. Washington, D.C.: The Brookings Institution, 1966.

Bos, H.C., and L.M. Koyck. "The Appraisal of Road Construction Projects: A Practical Example." *The Review of Economics and Statistics* 39, no. 3, 1957.

Currie, J.M., J.A. Murphy, and A. Schmitz. "The Concept of Economic Surplus and Its Use in Economic Analysis." *Economic Journal* 1971 (December).

Scott, M.F.G., J.D. MacArthur, and D.M.G. Newberry. *Project Appraisal in Practice.* London: Heinemann Educational Books, 1977.

7
Infrastructure Decisions in Fully Employed Economies

Two major difficulties arise when evaluating infrastructure projects (roads, subways, reservoirs, convention centers, or airports):

1. It is difficult to quantify many of the benefits because they are so far off in the future, and it is almost impossible to determine the complex interrelationships and net value added therefrom, including reductions in activity that would have otherwise developed in other sectors or regions. For example, one benefit of a large, new airport may be the time saved as compared with a preexisting smaller one for those now in the traffic stream. But what of the benefit for those whom the new airport, together with subsequent developments, might bring into the area in the first place, and for those future travelers who would never have faced the relative prices before the airport, and for whom it is meaningless to speak of a price reduction? What of the effect on alternative modes and their value added? How do we trace the impact of alternatives like video conferences? The problem has already been illustrated (problem 6.4).

2. Many of the benefits are nonmarket benefits—easier commutation, better water quality, noise abatement, and so on—and there may be no obvious way to introduce them into our national income benefit measurement framework. But an attempt to use consumer surplus for projects with such diverse effects is even more elusive and illusive.

We distinguish two situations: local projects and network projects. In practice, of course, few projects are exclusively one or the other. To exemplify the first, consider a bridge to replace a commuting ferry; to exemplify the second, a new link on a highway network.

Benefits of a Local Infrastructure Project

Imagine a bridge designed to replace a local ferry or to provide local commuter access as the city expands into new areas. There will probably also be some activity related to long-distance movement or tourism into the area and possibly some long-distance through movement as well. The diversity of the beneficiaries means that the benefits will be diverse: time savings, increased business for local shopkeepers, increases as well as declines in relative real estate values, savings in fuel for long-distance commutation, benefits of new recreational areas, reduction in ferry operating costs and/or relief of congestion on existing bridges, reduction of ferry profits, improved environment in new residential patterns, increased expenditure on automobiles and profits therefrom, and other impacts following as reactions to the initial project. How can all this possibly be summed up in a single measure?

We discuss two situations: in the first, the community has revenues (such as taxes) which it may invest in this project or use for any other purpose. This is not apt to be the situation where major capital works are involved. In the second, an agency—either the existing public sector organization or one established for the purpose—issues bonds to finance the project.

Investment Out of General Tax Revenues

The net benefit each year can be thought of as the difference between the total gross benefit and the cost. We follow our national accounting framework and look at the expenditure or use side of the accounts. The benefits include time savings, principally; any increase in safety (virtually impossible to judge, except possibly by reduction in liability insurance premiums by the ferry company); and reductions in operating costs in subsequent years. These reduced expenditures, in the fully employed economy, can be regarded as resource savings which may be directly reemployed.

Against these gross benefits we must compare the annual operating expenditures which will represent resource costs, since, in the fully employed economy, they must come from some other actual or imminent employment. The relevant items are shown in table 7–1. The difference then between B_t and C_t is the annual *virtual* net national income generation attributable to this project. We say "virtual" because is is not actually calculated by the national accounts office, but it has the same nature as many other nonmarket products and services, as we have previously noted several times.

Next, efficient pricing of this bridge requires that the isochronic cost element not be included in the price base: no congestion is remotely foreseen, and no parallel span is envisaged. Therefore, we need not view each bridge as the next unit of "production" in an expanding network linking a city to an opposite coast whose incremental cost must be reflected in user charges and collected from users. (Problem 7.3 provides an example with population growth and network expansion.) On the other hand, much of the initial investment is consumed according to various use measures—especially axle load— and must be assigned according to this use measure. Bridge painting is a pure time-variable cost and, in other circumstances, need not be recovered

Table 7-1
Benefits and Costs of Bridge Replacement of Ferry (Annual)

Benefits	Costs
1. Savings of cost of ferry operations, excluding depreciation	1. Time-variable cost, for example, bridge painting, snow removal
2. Ferry personal injury liability insurance premiums	2. Use-related costs, for example, pavement deterioration

3. Driver and passenger time by ferry
  a. for trips as intermediate production inputs—value at market wage
  b. for recreation and commutation trips—value at after-tax wage
	3. Driver and passenger time by bridge
	4. Toll booth operation
	5. Vehicle costs by bridge, including any cost of increased driving distance

4. Vehicle cost for ferry trips	

from users at all, since none of them influences the decision to paint. However, since the toll booth must be established in any event to collect for the incremental damage imposed, this time-variable joint cost might as well be recovered also in order to avoid any untoward income distribution to the higher-income groups (to which automobile commuters, by and large, belong), or, equally, to forestall comparable demands by others, causing an undue burden on public revenue.

The question for the project decision is whether the difference between the gross benefit and the cost is big enough. Assuming that the annual net benefit is constant from year to year, the first requirement we must impose is that this annual benefit not be less than the opportunity cost or productivity of the funds employed, that is, the return on the best alternative use of the funds in the public or private sectors. But this is not enough, since, for example, if d is the annual productivity and the net annual benefit is just equal to dI_i, the investment will not be exceeded by the benefits if the life of the project is too short. However, if the difference is large enough and the project life long enough, it may be justified. Since the productivity of capital is d (assumed), the invested funds I_i would be worth $(1 + d)^T I_i$ at the end of T years. Hence, only if the total benefit, if reinvested, were worth at least this much at the end of T_i years would it be justified. In other words, our basic investment criterion $\sum_{t=0}^{T_i} R_{it}(1 + d)^{-t}$, may be applied (problem 7.4). Note, furthermore, that even without population growth in the area, there is bound to be some growth in traffic following a fall in crossing cost simply because demand curves slope downward. In this case the consumer surplus triangle may be added into the calculation of the net benefit, although it is likely to be very small and not substantially affect benefit estimation. This is deferred to chapter 9 (problem 9.4).

One may ask why the productivity rule should apply since the funds are in the budget anyway (they already belong to the public sector). The answer is that we are working within the framework of social welfare maximization, not of spending public monies; if a public-sector investment cannot do at least as well as the lowest-ranked alternative private-sector investment, we should not want the funds to flow to the public sector in the first place. Naturally, if the expenditures in question are (justifiably) designed for income distribution objectives, this comment does not apply.

Special Bond Issues

The net benefits of a project may be extremely difficult to pin down. Consider, for example, the vehicle operating cost saving on the cost side of the balance sheet of our previous example. Suppose there is independently generated growth in the city region and, hence, growth in the population pool from which the traffic will be drawn. What meaning can we attach to the cost of driving on the bridge for a newcomer to the area whose gain is not recorded on the benefit side? How can his net utility gain be measured? How can his change of lifestyle possibly be summed up in this table? If it cannot, the only way we can hope to find out whether the project is justified will be by seeing whether the total cost is recovered. This may be thought of as a profit criterion: if it is possible to recover all costs, including opportunity cost, given a zero economic profit, the project is worthwhile, and we may think of ourselves as following a profit maximizing criterion. Unfortunately, it is not possible to calculate this until many years after the bridge is in operation, because the planner cannot conceive of the host of impacts and feedbacks into the traffic stream, not to speak of the benefits to be derived by persons not now even remotely foreseen. As problem 7.4 shows, the longer the life of the project, the more uncertain the returns owing to possible relative price changes; and the more wrenching the presumed effects, the greater is the need for market information provided by revenue bond financing.

In such situations the only reasonable approach is through bond financing, with the payback limited to receipts from the immediate activity. The project will not be undertaken if the bonds are not sold. Moreover, the effective interest rate depends on the bond price. Thus, the evaluation of the economic rationality of the decision will not be the exclusive domain of the planner, but must be agreed upon by the market. The individual investors are in effect asked to make a judgment about people's need for the bridge, just as they would for a private-sector investment decision. Indeed, the lines between public-sector and private-sector activities are sufficiently fuzzy so that even today a new light rail line in the Dallas–Fort Worth area has recently been proposed for joint undertaking by the public sector and private developer. This practice is to be encouraged in contrast to the usual expectation today that the public sector will do it. In this case what is necessary is to make sure the ground rules conduce to optimal decisions.

This decision framework might be instituted through the use of revenue bonds issued by an agency specifically set up for the project with repayment of interest and principal expressly related to the project and explicitly disavowed by the parent state or province.

One frequent objection to this approach is that repayment requires revenue collection, which requires use of additional resources, while at the same time the users of the facility impose no incremental resource cost on the system, thus implying a net social cost: since any user with a positive demand price, however close to zero, will gain more than the cost he imposes, to prohibit use reduces the social gain from the facility (problem 3.16). This argument is weakened substantially by the recognition that much of the initial investment expense goes for components which will wear out with some measure of use (for example, rails, pavement surface). Moreover, these use dimensions are often reflected in subdemand curves (such as different vehicle classes) which can provide a basis for differential or discriminatory pricing, and full cost can be recovered with a minimum of inefficient denial of use (problem 7.5). For projects with investment components which are less use-variable, dams or power lines for example, there also exist subdemand curves—daytime, afternoon, or evening; bulk versus small users—which can provide a basis for efficient price discrimination. At the same time, as explained in chapter 9, consumer surplus, often advocated as the efficiency criterion for such situations, suffers several weaknesses: when there are changes in the basic environment of the sort necessary to stimulate enough traffic to justify the project, the criterion breaks down because a single demand curve cannot be assumed to prevail before and after; and when traffic growth is small, the consumer surplus is not likely to yield a positive net benefit measure although the future population may value the project in relation to its evolving location, income, and price structure.

There is a second objection against the revenue bond and full-cost recovery approach: if it is true that the public-sector investments tend to have rates of capital productivity below those of the private sector, but still above the social rate of time preference (which we argued to be the case in chapter 5), how can revenue bond financing ensure that such lower return projects will be accepted if their bonds must compete on the same market as other financial investment instruments, including shares of private industrial corporations? This objection can be answered in the following way.

Many of the private-sector investments after the event do have very high returns, but many also generate low returns—below those on relatively riskless public ventures. This is an ex-post statement. Thus, in the language of chapter 5, while the ex-ante or expected intertemporal consumption frontier is less bent, with the public sector projects close to the Y-axis, the ex-post frontier is decidedly more curved, with many private-sector projects to the right of public-sector ones. If it turned out that the public-sector projects were also risky, they would be further from the Y-axis on the ex-ante curve, and, after the fact, some might have a higher payoff, and others a lower payoff, possibly even a loss. There seems to be no good reason for insisting that things be otherwise and that some sort of subsidy or preferential tax treatment should be given to the public-sector investment to ensure that a lower rate of interest could be secured for the public project. While we argued earlier that some public-sector projects should be discounted at a lower rate which, we believe, corresponds to the equilibrium social discount rate, those projects were relatively risk free—a ferry-replacing bridge that would reduce total travel costs for existing traffic (including the little "generated" traffic within the present population that might result from the investment). But a project whose impact is more speculative, depending as it does on a host of consequences not at all related to the project, should be evaluated at the appropriate risk-adjusted rate which will be higher and close to that of private sector projects of comparable risk.

The foregoing view is then inconsistent with the present procedure for revenue bonds issued by subfederal public-sector agencies, such as project execution authorities in the United States. There, although not in Canada or elsewhere, interest on such bonds is exempt from federal income tax, so for an investor in the 60-percent incremental tax bracket, a bond coupon rate of 5 percent corresponds to a 12.5 percent return on ordinary bonds (for example, private-sector industrial bonds, federal bonds, or treasury bills) and is clearly preferred for equal risk even to bonds bearing a pretax coupon rate twice as high. This is a clear pricing distortion. Moreover, even though the payback funds are nominally limited to project revenues, and the responsibility for repayment by the parent public-sector organ is expressly disavowed, the possibility of such intervention is not absolutely precluded. This reinforces the first distortion as a source of misdirection of investment. The increasing use of such revenue bonds by state or municipal districts to establish industrial parks to attract private business is a further example of a distorting subsidy.

Given the investment distortion implicit in the use of tax-exempt revenue bonds, we realize that the execution of a project today should not be decided by analogy with the physical results of earlier projects undertaken elsewhere. That is to say, for a situation being studied today, nothing can be inferred from the fact that traffic growth following a bridge on some other route was 50 percent: crossing costs may actually have fallen (in toll alone, not to speak of combined toll and time saving), although opportunity costs (including depreciation) are substantially higher. This represents the kind of socially inefficient demand of which we have spoken so much. Consumer surplus arguments cannot be used either, since the underlying demand curves may be so different, as we will show in chapter 9.

We note that, in contrast to revenue bonds, general financial obligations issued by public sector units, such as school districts, which also are exempt from federal taxes, cannot be rejected as categorically as the revenue bonds. These bonds require repayment from general tax revenues of the taxing authority, and many have an income distribution intent. Their backing by the tax base provides reduced risk and also imposes a greater responsibility on the issuing agency vis-a-vis its constituents. It is still possible that their reduced rate in the United States, as compared with industrial bonds of equal risk—utility bonds, say—distorts investment patterns, however.

In summary, revenue bonds for toll roads, bridges, ferries, public-sector power provision, and numerous other activities in principle constitute a way to decide on public sector investments whose beneficiaries are now unknown. They represent a way to get the most information on a project, namely the evaluations of potential investors as to its ability to recover its costs. Given the existence of numerous dimensions of demand for these activities and the fact that different incremental cost patterns are associated with them, which, in any event, requires imposition of payment collection mechanisms, we expect that a reasonably efficient method for recovering isochronic and time-variable costs can also be imposed. But we note that the level of these costs may be too low because an opportunity cost on the funds was set too low in the first place through exemption of the bonds from federal income taxes.

Network Projects

The consummate example of a network project is an addition to a highway grid. Other examples include a network of bridge connections to a city, such as those managed by the Authority of the Port of New York and New Jersey or the Triborough Bridge and Tunnel Authority in the greater New York region, for which we may think of each bridge or tunnel as being one more link in the set of transfluvial connections. Network expansions should be financed either through bond issues not necessarily restricted to any particular link (rather than by earmarked revenue bonds, with total revenues of the authority available to discharge any of the obligations), or by currently generated user charge revenues. In either case the investment and operating budgets should be closely tied to the use of the facility. Accordingly, the first problem to investigate is whether or not an efficient budget constraint may be assumed to exist. This requires analysis of the structure of user charges in the sector. We emphasize that when using the road network as an example, we are talking about the basic road network itself, although there may be isolated stretches of road which primarily serve an income distribution function. For example, a major road in Appalachia, even if nominally a part of the Interstate Highway System, might be evaluated on the basis of income distribution criteria, competing with other potential projects in that region. Other

116 • *Project Decision Making in the Public Sector*

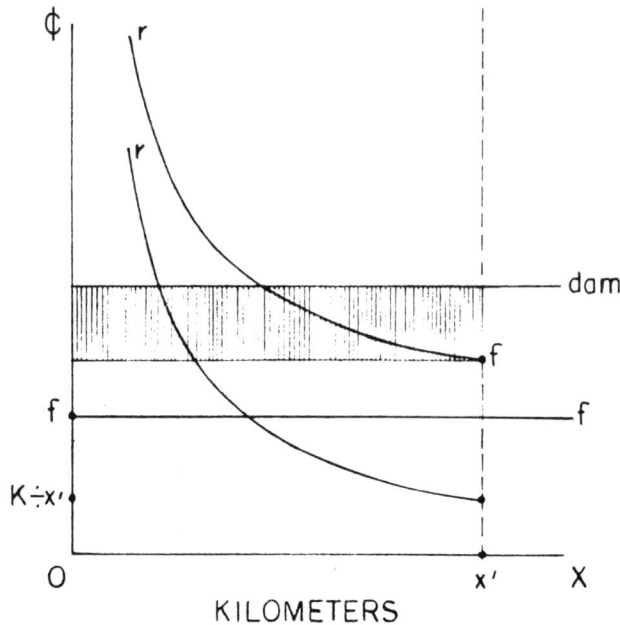

Figure 7-1. Typical Cost Curves for a Large Truck of Given Configuration and Load (Showing Net Social Cost and Annual Volume x^1)

examples are the Transamazon highway or the Belem–Brasilia highway in Brazil.

It is this writer's experience that almost no country has an efficient budget constraint for its highway sector. There are usually two sources of distortion: (1) there is a transfer from urban users to the intercity network, and (2) there is a subsidy of large trucks by small ones and by automobiles. In the usual situation the picture is something like figure 7-1, which shows the essential cost behavior for large trucks and the taxes per mile paid by a truck of given configuration and load. The curve is typical for large trucks. The average fuel tax is given by the straight line *ff,* and the average annual registration fee by the hyperbola *rr*. The damage imposed by the vehicle every mile is the straight line *dam*. An estimate of this damage could be based on the road tests conducted by the American Association of State Highway Officials, which have already been cited several times. Recall that the relative damage coefficients of two axle loads are proportional to the fourth power of the weight ratio. The curve *rf* is the private cost per ton-mile, the sum of *rr* and *ff*. Assuming that for this truck the demand for the road is such that it justifiably is asked to make no contribution to the isochronic cost component, and that all its user charges are properly applied against output-variable cost elements, the net social cost is given by the area between the *rf* and *dam* curves up to any level of output, here assumed to be x'.

The damage cost line, *dam,* in figure 7–1 reflects only the ascribable damage which could be avoided if the truck did not pass. In this allocation we are assigning nothing to the truck for the isochronic cost elements—the basic grading, culverts, bridges, and so on, or even for joint annual maintenance such as snow removal. In spite of this it is safe to say that for almost all vehicles of gross vehicle weight greater than twenty tons, the user charges would be higher if they were based on ASSHO coefficients. In America some states are beginning to impose such user charges related to incremental damage imposition through the so-called third-structure taxes.

Note that if trucks were to pay only according to this incremental damage, there would remain a large road expenditure component—the initial isochronic investment expenditure and some of the annual time-variable joint costs such as snow removal. These should be priced according to the intensity of demand, much, or most, of it coming from the smaller trucks and automobiles. However, we repeat the admonition that city use constitutes a very different activity, quite unrelated to intercity use, and the taxes generated therein (including part of the annual registration fees) should be kept distinct from the intercity budget.

If the road authority did have an efficient-budget constraint, how should it allocate its investment expenditure? Note that, with the correct prices, total annual expenditure would be covered: the annual investment expenditure would be determined by the amount of use desired by the high-demand traffic components. How and where the investment should take place are questions which remain to be answered.

The existence of so many interrelationships—between movement and location, between movement on different roads, between movement by road and movement by rail, or between movement in different size vehicles—virtually precludes any attempt to measure the net national income change resulting from a particular stretch of road. (However, for an isolated, non-network, road or settlement project which includes a road, national income is calculable by the examples of chapter 8.) Accordingly, the desirability of different road stretches should be evaluated in terms of time savings and/or savings of material inputs. Typically, the greatest opportunities for savings will arise on the most traveled subnetworks, so these will grow fastest through greater internal ramification. Their greater use indicates greater potential benefit, but it is to be expected that in some years little expansion will be called for in some regions even though they are generating revenue through their high-demand traffic components. To some extent we can envisage the whole process as a sort of interregional loan operation, with some regions "lending" money for investment out of their revenues and receiving repayment in the form of additional connections within their regions in later years. (Incidentally, the "rule of 72" provides a quick way to estimate various growth attainments, given arbitrary growth rates (problem 7.6)).

This whole procedure appears distinctly unambitious when compared with the hopes of formulating a cost-benefit project decision criterion isolated from the issues of financing and pricing of services. It especially runs counter to the earlier hopes that consumer surplus might present a good approach. Chapter 9 will help us to understand some of the specific weaknesses of consumer surplus for this purpose.

Even though working on its own, the road authority still may have to discount over the future, since the alternatives which it faces at any time will involve different streams of savings and costs. What rate of discount should be used? Indeed, should net present value or internal rate of return be used? It probably does not matter very much. There is certainly an inconsistency in using either one to the extent that the returns generated may have no reinvestability: automobile time savings, for example, cannot be reinvested, while common carrier time savings can be. Yet the choice between IRR and NPV is probably much less important than the question of whether or not the budget constraint is efficient (generated by correctly designed user charges). We believe that far too little attention has been given to this issue.

Problems

7.1 Two cities are separated by a channel across which transportation is now provided by year-round ferry service. A bridge is being considered. The ferries had a twenty-five-year life when new, and are fifteen years old. Annual ferry operating costs are as follows:

Fuel	$800,000
Personnel (including crew, maintenance, and administration)	2,000,000
Depreciation (straight-line basis)	1,600,000
Rent of office, harbor facilities, and so on	950,000
Miscellaneous	625,000

Consider two situations and determine the benefit in the form of ferry cost savings for each:

1. The channel is a freshwater, shallow river, which imposes certain design requirements on the vessel. There are no nearby cities and vessels could not safely make an ocean trip;
2. The channel is salt water with access to the ocean.

Solution

1. For the first ten years of the bridge operation, we must count as a benefit all potential ferry expenditures which are avoided. In the first year of operation this will be $4,375,000 (excluding depreciation) plus the net scrap value of the ferries, probably around $2,000,000 in total. The ferry cost benefit in subsequent years will also be $4,375,000.

2. Now the ferries have a resale value. Under the assumed conditions it will be $16,000,000. Therefore, in the first year the benefit will be $20,375,000; in each of the next nine years, $4,375,000.

In both cases the one-time recovery may be used to help pay for the bridge construction.

7.2. Now assume expenditures are as in 7.1, but inflation in the shipbuilding industry since the ferries were built has been 65 percent. There have been no technological improvements. Make the respective calculations.

Solution

1. Inflation will affect all prices, including intermediate inputs (scrap steel) and labor, which affects scrapping cost. Hence, the scrap value should be $3,300,000. Note: Equal industry-wide inflation is suggested by the statement that there are no technological improvements. If we know that steel prices in the economy have risen only 35 percent, say, the scrap value would rise only $700,000 to $2,700,000 (assuming all scrap value to derive from steel scrap).

2. The ferry resale value is now $26,400,000.

7.3. Now suppose that the cities on both banks in 7.1 are expanding apace. One bridge has already been built, and another is being considered. Show the consequences of failing to include depreciation in the price base for the bridges.

Solution

Recall the congestion analysis of chapter 4 (problem 4.3). The corresponding curves for the one-bridge and two-bridge situations are shown in figure 7P-1. ASC and MSC reflect only vehicle operating costs, excluding any and all bridge costs.

The isochronic cost component of the bridge, per vehicle, may be thought of as an attempt to approximate the correct congestion toll ($MSC - ASC$) at optimal congestion.

The isochronic component may fail to equal exactly the optimal toll, but it is impossible to accept or refute such a claim since the congestion analysis is an abstraction whose demand and cost curves cannot be precisely specified. But we do know that if no congestion toll is imposed, there will be a social inefficiency, which we exemplify by the shaded areas in figure 7P–1.

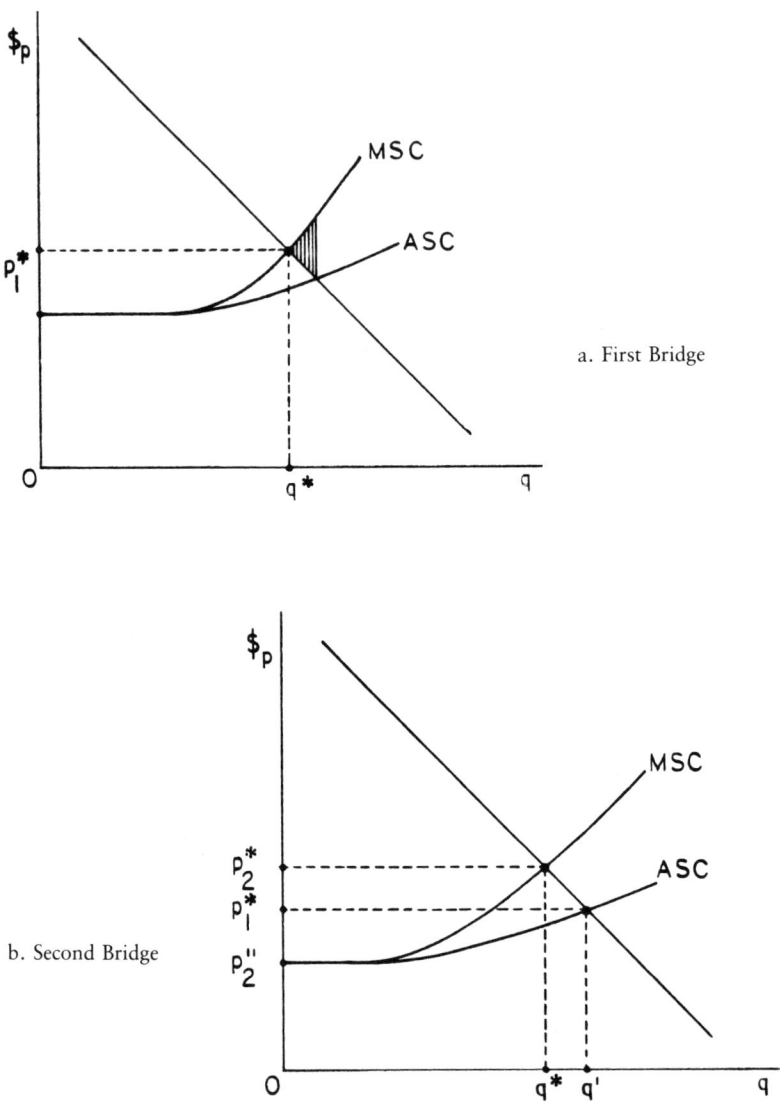

Figure 7P–1. Analysis of Congestion for Bridge Situation

Now, if the new bridge price does not include the isochronic component, there will be a surge of traffic to this route with inefficient congestion at traffic level q', which is where demand price p_1^* is equal to ASC. We do not, however, know the shape of the ASC and MSC functions, partly because we do not even know the traffic composition, or how the toll itself induces variations in traffic distribution.

But in the absence of such information, can we say that it is better to build bridges large enough to eliminate all congestion? Certainly not. Rather, one bridge is built today; a toll equal to $p_2^* - \text{ASC}(q^*)$ is charged to cover the cost, and approximate MSC-ASC at optimal traffic level, and as traffic builds up over the years it generates revenue to help build a subsequent connection. Otherwise there is a danger that the economy will react to physical measures (traffic growth, delay time) which may constitute allocatively inefficient demand. Moreover, burdens would then be placed on local highway networks and on urban facilities in the outlying areas, which, once the precedent of responding to physical measures is confirmed, will stimulate investments in these activities, which may also be inefficient. If isochronic costs are removed from all bridges, they will all experience inefficient traffic levels unless enough capacity is provided (more bridges or bigger) to allow them to operate where the cost curves are horizontal (so that $MSC = ASC$). If the new bridge includes a toll equal to $p_2^* - \text{ASC}(q^*)$, traffic will be optimal. This is evidently true by theoretic considerations. One *hopes* that it will be approximated by the unit isochronic cost component of the toll to be charged.

7.4. The following data relate to a ferry replacement problem with no traffic growth. They are all annual figures (millions of dollars). The bridge would cost $60,000,000.

Cost of ferry operations (excludes depreciation)	8.5
Depreciation of ferries	1.6
Ferry personal liability insurance	0.1
Time of passengers (correctly valued)	4.0
Vehicle cost (idling, starting, extra distances traveled from origin)	1.2
Time-variable bridge upkeep	2.3
Vehicle-variable deterioration	3.9
Time of passengers	1.2
Tollbooth operation	2.5
Vehicle costs (extra travel distances)	4.0

The bridge would last at least fifty years. The ferries, which cost $20,000,000 when new fifteen years ago, have ten years of life remaining. Their residual value would be entirely as scrap ($2,000,000)(the resale situation is that of problem 7.1.1). There is no inflation and none is expected. Should the project be undertaken?

Solution

We first classify the data into benefits and costs. Note that while ferry depreciation and vehicle-variable road costs are critical factors for pricing, they are not treated as part of the annual stream. Rather, cash flow *type* projections are employed (see problem 5.13). This will lead to an extra bridge benefit of $20,000,000 in the tenth year ($t = 9$) in the form of an expenditure on ferry replacement which as avoided by having the bridge instead (this is cash saved). On the other hand, we must also deduct from the net benefit the cost of road surfacing (and repair of other vehicle-related damage, such as weakening of spars caused by traffic vibrations), which is assumed to take place every ten years at a cost of $8,000,000. Table 7P-1 shows the annual net benefits unadjusted and discounted at three different rates (3 percent, 5 percent, and 7 percent). Although the bridge is certainly expected to last fifty years with proper upkeep, we calculate benefits only for the first thirty years on the ground that benefits thereafter are rather uncertain owing to, for example, the changing relative valuations which may raise or lower the value of time.

Table 7P-1
Net Benefit Stream of Bridge Option

Year (t)	R_{it} ($ millions)	Net Present Value		
		$d = .03$	$d = .05$	$d = .07$
0	-58.0	-58.00	-58.00	-58.00
1	3.8	3.69	3.62	3.55
2	3.8	3.58	3.45	3.32
3	3.8	3.48	3.29	3.10
4	3.8	3.37	3.13	2.90
5	3.8	3.28	2.98	2.71
6	3.8	3.19	2.84	2.53
7	3.8	3.10	2.71	2.36
8	3.8	3.01	2.58	2.21
9	23.8	18.30	15.35	8.35
10	-5.2	-3.89	-3.19	-2.64
11	3.8	2.75	2.22	1.80
12	3.8	2.67	2.12	1.68
13	3.8	2.59	2.02	1.58
14	3.8	2.52	1.92	1.47
15	3.8	2.44	1.83	1.37
16	3.8	2.37	1.74	1.28
17	3.8	2.30	1.66	1.20
18	3.8	2.24	1.58	1.12
19	3.8	2.17	1.50	1.05

Table 7P-1 (continued)

Year (t)	R_{it} ($ millions)	Net Present Value		
		$d = .03$	$d = .05$	$d = .07$
20	−5.2	−2.89	−1.95	−1.43
21	3.8	2.04	1.36	0.92
22	3.8	1.98	1.30	0.86
23	3.8	1.92	1.24	0.80
24	3.8	1.87	1.18	0.75
25	3.8	1.81	1.12	0.70
26	3.8	1.76	1.07	0.65
27	3.8	1.71	1.02	0.61
28	3.8	1.66	0.97	0.57
29	3.8	1.61	0.92	0.53
$\sum_{t=1}^{29} R_{it}(1+d)^{-t}$		76.63	53.35	45.90
add $R_0 = -I$		18.63	−4.65	−12.10
Present Value				
Residual Value: Bridge	24.0	10.21	5.82	3.37
Salvage Value: Ferries	4.0	1.70	0.97	0.56
Net Residual Value:	20.0	8.51	4.85	2.81
Net Present Value		27.15	0.20	−9.29

After thirty years the residual value of the ferries purchased in the tenth year is taken to be one-fifth of their purchase price, since they would be expected to have five more years of life. This value is discounted and subtracted from the earlier cumulative stream. (It is subtracted because it represents a benefit that would have arisen if the ferry technology had been maintained. This benefit is sacrificed by introducing the bridge technology.) Similarly, the residual value of the bridge at that time ($24,000,000 on a straight-line depreciation basis) is discounted and added to the stream on the ground that it will continue to have a value for the community. The discounted present values are shown with a breakdown by major component (flows over the first twenty-nine years of operation, capital expenditure, and discounted residual value) in the bottom few lines. The total flow discounted only at 3 percent is positive; discounting at 5 percent is negative before allowing for the residual value of the bridge (at which point it becomes barely positive); discounting at 7 percent gives an NPV of −9.29 million.

Should the bridge be undertaken?

We note how sensitive the value of the project is to the assumed residual value of the bridge in its thirtieth year and to the discount rate. Moreover, during the thirtieth year, another $8 million must be spent on road restoration. Since the bridge is known to be able to survive for twenty more years (it had an original fifty-year life), it could be argued that benefits should be calculated for the next two decades, discounted, and added to the NPV. However, relative values of time and other inputs and outputs may change unpredictably during these years, so we would not be on very firm ground if we did so. On the other hand, of course, since ultimately the residual value must derive from the future benefit stream, the end-year value arrived at by straight-line depreciation is itself, at best, a guess. Given the small NPV, however, it would seem unwise to proceed unless we are quite convinced that 3 percent is the correct rate. This might be the case if the investment is relatively small, so we can feel that we will not be cutting into investments with a higher return. One possible approach would be to consider revenue bond financing to let the market help in our decision.

It is very probable that for such a large project a loan would have to be secured in any event (the ferries themselves were probably financed in that way). This would undoubtedly require a higher bond price (or, equivalently, a higher rate of discount). This is proper, since we would now be cutting back into the pool of potential private investment which is lent out at higher interest rates (recall the analysis of chapter 5). In effect we would be asking investors what they believed about the potential returns from the bridge to private individuals. These returns would be manifested in a willingness to pay tolls to contribute to the bond amortization. The required rate would undoubtedly be considerably higher than 5 percent, and the bond market would probably find against the project; note that in column 5 the NPV is calculated on the basis of a 7 percent discount rate and the NPV based on thirty years is negative ($-\$9.29$ million).

Finally, this whole approach is limited to situations in which relatively little traffic change is expected. But it might well be the case that expenditures under the bridge option would exceed those of the ferry technology: since more people will travel by bridge, the total cost of operations and time will exceed that of the ferries; therefore, subtracting bridge costs from ferry costs would yield negative cost differences throughout! But the reason for high vehicle and time inputs by bridge is that many people want to use it, and this fact must indicate something about social desirability. Being unable to determine and commensurate everyone's preferences through any other means, however, we must let the market decide. In this situation the best way is a revenue bond issue with amortization payments related to users' toll payments.

An obvious objection to the market test approach is that the construction decision can be made only after the bonds are sold. The market may react unfavorably by insisting on a higher interest rate (lower bond price), yielding total proceeds below the target for construction and requiring higher tolls, which may have an impact on traffic and/or force revision of traffic projections. But it is certainly preferable to determine this now and either provide in advance for contingent sale of bonds, with whatever transaction expenses are required, than to commit general tax revenues to a project which might turn out to have negative real social benefit.

Finally, we should be reminded that this problem assumes zero traffic growth to simplify exposition, help us to concentrate on the classification of costs and benefits, and see the effect of different discount rates. The project with traffic growth would warrant investigation of revenue bonds and the rate of growth would be critical in determining the ability to repay. A good idea of the absolute growth implied by various rates of growth is given by the "rule of 72" in problem 7.6.

7.5. Suppose there are just two traffic classes, and time-incremental resource costs are zero. We still need to control entry, however, because it will be necessary to charge each user the variable cost (a function of the user's weight and configuration) he imposes on the system. For each user draw a demand curve and a variable cost-adjusted demand curve (that is, a demand curve displaced toward the origin by shifting it vertically downward by the amount of the variable cost which it must pay; this shows the ability of that class to contribute to joint costs).

In the usual formulation traffic is physically homogeneous, and there is no way to apportion the joint cost, either time-variable incremental joint cost or amortization of isochronic components; people do, of course, place different values on the service, or else the demand curve would not slope downward, but there is no obvious way to discover these demands. For this case the alternative to payment of "marginal cost" (here, only the traffic variable cost) is assumed to be payment of average cost (including joint costs). This is believed to be inefficient as compared with the usually presumed Dupuit solution.

Show that with discrimination made possible by the existence of two vehicle classes, the deviation from consumer surplus maximization may be small, that is, there will be a minimal denial of passage. Assume that the annual joint time-variable cost and isochronic cost allowance is $400. (The entire isochronic cost will eventually be recovered from users.)

Solution

Figure 7P–2a shows the traditional analysis. The average cost curve (for the time-variable joint costs and the amortization of isochronic cost component only) is a rectangular hyperbola. The inefficiency is the shaded area. Discrimination to recover full cost is not possible because collection costs are high, and/or the demands of individual users cannot be determined. Therefore, it is recommended that vehicles pass free of charge.

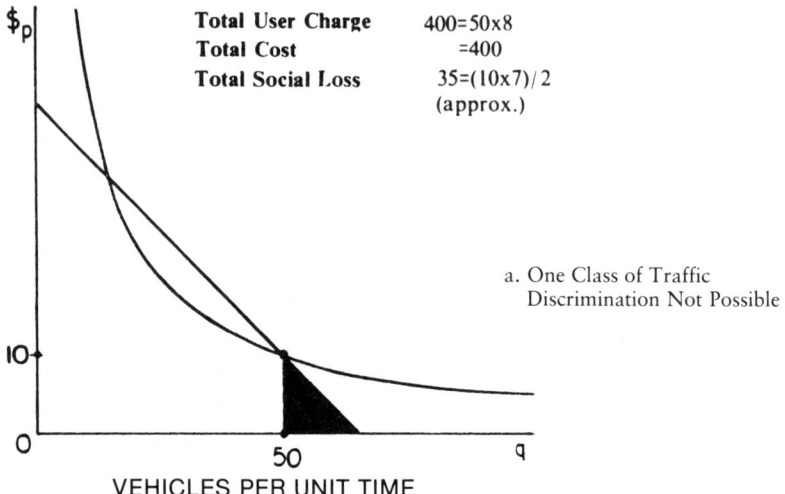

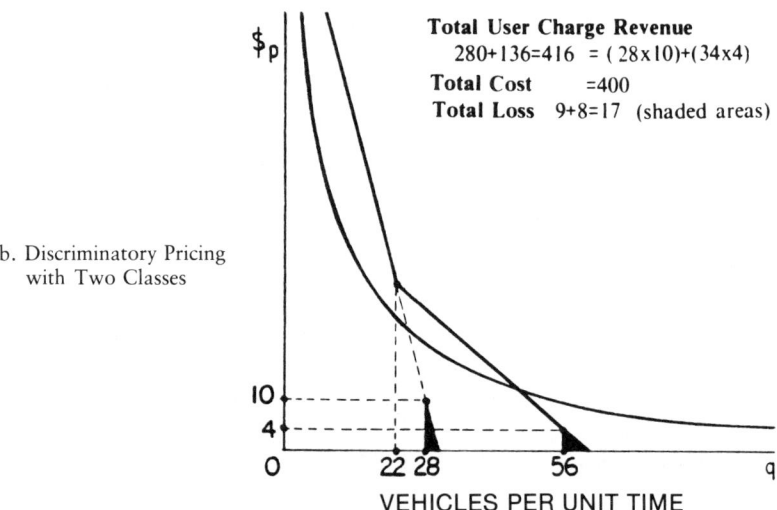

Figure 7P–2. Deadweight Loss when Discrimination Is Not Possible and When Discrimination Is Possible

Figure 7P–2b shows the two-class traffic situation. The individual traffic demands are shown together with the total market demand (all in vehicles). Remember: these joint costs, by definition, cannot be ascribed to individual users except on the basis of demand-related discrimination. Note also that in any event, since some way must be devised to cover the directly variable cost, the inability-to-discriminate argument loses part of its force, and the collection-cost argument loses all of its force.

There are many time-variable cost allocations which may be used to recover total cost. One possibility is shown in figure 7P–2b. Evidently, the shortfall (shaded area) is small.

Incidentally, although Dupuit was the first to use consumer surplus to illustrate efficient pricing, he never showed cost curves in his graphic analyses. This implies that he was unable to satisfactorily reconcile the different dimensions of cost, or else he believed that no costs varied with respect to any dimension (time, axle load, number of vehicles). This is discussed further in chapter 9. However, as noted there, he also added the qualification that a positive price should be charged if an annual expense, such as interest or maintenance cost (implicitly assumed to be time variable) was to be covered.

7.6. The Rule of 72 may be useful if you find yourself in the middle of the jungle with no calculator handy. This rule enables you to calculate the time necessary for an amount to double at any assumed growth rate: put the growth rate in percentage terms and divide it into 72. The quotient gives the number of years required to double. Find the error in the approximation for growth rates of .02, .06, .10, and .20.

Solution

Table 7P–2
Comparison of True Growth and "Rule of 72" Estimates

	Rate			
	.02	.06	.10	.20
No. of years to double by Rule of 72	36.0	12.0	7.2	3.6
Actual compound growth during this time period (%)	104.0	101.2	98.0	92.8
Error as percentage of true growth	4.0	1.2	−2.0	−7.8

8
Project Decisions in the Underdeveloped Economy

The less-than-fully-employed (LTFE) framework embraces both the developing or unindustrialized economy (apart from its fully employed regions, if any) and the secularly unemployed regions of the developed countries. The major concern is usually the former, however, and this will be the assumed context, although we emphasize that the fully employed regions or sectors of such an economy should have their investment decision rules based on procedures and criteria discussed earlier.

The public sector will use its funds for direct investment in projects and for subsidies and loans to SOEs; it may even cooperate in privately held firms through loans or equity participation. The main substantive difference in policy between the unindustrialized and the industrialized economies is the greater activity in investments related to distribution and efficiency. These include agricultural, agro-industrial, training, and similar projects, where there is an important distribution component in the absorption of underemployed labor, as well as an efficiency goal as measured by national income change. This substantive difference translates into the main difference in procedure—that is, it is necessary to calculate national income change by complete enumeration rather than through cost reduction or other surrogate measures. The main differences in the interpretation of the various measures are the subject of the first section of this chapter.

Furthermore, in an unindustrialized economy there is a much greater expectation that shadow adjustments are necessary. Indeed, it would be no exaggeration to say that the key to rational project decision making in the developing country context *is* the analysis of shadow values. All of the issues discussed in chapters 4 and 5 are relevant: the essence or nature of import duties, the value of labor, the value of physical assets, the impact of inflation on the measurement of prices and costs, the marginal productivity of capital, and the social rate of discount. In those chapters the major conclusion was that adjustments should not be introduced in an absolute or across-the-board way, and great care must be exercised in each particular situation to decide whether an adjustment from market values is called for. A number of problems are cited later (see also problems 6.7–6.9) to exemplify the necessary considerations.

Relationships among Benefit Measures

In chapter 6 we looked at the interrelationships among reasonable measures of benefit within the context of the secularly fully employed economy. The measures were all rectangular. Consumer surplus was not considered because it was not believed to be appropriate. The reasons for this will be examined in some detail in chapter 9. Some commonly used performance measures, most notably profit and cost reduction, were seen to be equivalent to national income, and these obviated the need to trace all the impacts on national income itself.

When it comes to the developing economy context, however, only growth of real national income or real consumption, among rectangular measures, can be taken *necessarily* to imply improved welfare. In particular, cost reduction and profit movements imply nothing about the direction of welfare change or about national income change. The reason is that costs *might* be reduced or profits increased by dismissing workers, and, with the declining marginal utility of income a lower welfare level is suggested. On the other hand, profits *might* rise through reduction of nonlabor costs, which *might* lead to higher real income and welfare.

Consumption does continue to be positively associated with welfare, but now it is also positively associated with national income growth, while in the fully employed economy, consumption can be increased only at the expense of investment, with indeterminate final impact on national income: the relationship is indeterminate since increasing consumption, rather than investment, between this year and next might lead to a lower income next year, or it might not. Change in real national income is positively associated with welfare changes in both economies. Moreover, focusing on real national income itself rather than the surrogates also enables us to resolve most of the issues involved in the shadow pricing of labor for the underemployed economy. Projects that are more labor intensive generate a greater national income benefit, all other things equal, because they assimilate unemployed labor into the labor force. This narrows income inequality, obviating the need for a vector-valued benefit measure based on output and some distributional characteristics. Of course, it has precisely the effect advocated by proponents of opportunity-cost pricing for labor; that is, when labor is in excess supply with an opportunity cost less than the market wage, it should be priced at this opportunity cost. Thus, labor-intensive projects would tend to be preferred, all other things equal (problem 8.1). Similarly, if a worker is already employed, but is earning more than his potential product in his best alternative employment, we want the lower wage to be used for project decisions which use that industry as a source of intermediate inputs. For example, suppose a strong teamsters' union manages to hold driver wages above opportunity costs. How should the trucking input to a new project be treated? Again, concentrating on real national income will resolve the dilemma: since recorded cost is used as a basis for pricing in national income calculations, the national income change originating in the project will be based on the market wage, thus enhancing the measure of this project and satisfying an income distribution goal (problem 8.2).

Shadow Values

While reference to national income calculations will often obviate the need to shadow price low-skilled or excess labor in certain circumstances, the need for a shadow valuation may sometimes arise. One approach is to apply across-the-board coefficients or "national parameters," such as .5 for the real cost of unskilled labor and .75 for semiskilled, to determine the true labor cost of the project. However, since conditions in a country may vary greatly among regions, we urge that the specific local opportunity costs be determined instead (problems 8.3 and 8.4).

One reason for urging closer examination of specific conditions is to uncover secondary impacts. For example, if a farm worker produces 30 percent of what he would earn in a prospective industrial enterprise, it is possible that his net contribution to national income will not be only 70 percent of his industrial earnings. By investigating the project labor sources, it may be found that his agricultural production can still be produced by another family member, possibly even himself by working evenings and weekends.

National parameters are sometimes urged for transportation services. In the usual approach, however, a single value, frequently less than 1.0, is used, but this is invalid because of the dependence of transport cost on use dimensions, most notably axle weight for highway transport. Thus, at a minimum, any serious project study should attempt to discern the probable traffic distribution accompanying the project and use cost adjustments appropriate to the anticipated traffic classes. However, insistence on redesigning highway user charges for general market use is better, since shippers at existing plants, as well as new investments, must take account of true costs. Railroad and other transport prices should also be reviewed if, as is often the case, there exist large subsidies which cannot be justified in terms of distributional or national–political objectives. Several illustrations of this problem have already been provided.

One major reason for pressing for user charge reform is our belief that most network type activities should be financed through correct user charges.

132 • *Project Decision Making in the Public Sector*

Too often, roads are believed to have a disproportionate potential for contributing to the economy, and, since their benefits are supposed to extend far beyond the private gains of the users, a less-than-full-cost recovery user charge structure is espoused. This is inefficient and, usually, inequitable, as the higher-income groups gain disproportionately. Therefore, the intranetwork loan financing and project choice procedure, as described in chapter 7, should be employed as in the fully employed economy. This does not preclude the financing of some apparently network-related, but essentially separable, investments out of general tax revenues, as in the developed economy: there may be distribution-related road projects, as part of a regional development scheme, which should be treated as part of a complex project not related to the network user charge efficient-budget constraint, as exemplified by problem 8.4.

By now some readers may be tired of exhortations for correctly designed user charges to generate an efficient budget constraint allowing for expansion of the network—highways, power grids, bridge connections, or pipelines—and they may be demanding decision rules based on the more realistic recognition that user charges *are not* correct, and to await their rationalization as a prelude to action will assure that nothing will be done. However, in a book dealing with optimal project decision making, to do less than insist on better pricing structures and to pretend that we can go straight to correct decisions in the presence of pricing inefficiency is even more unrealistic. Hence, the rule we espouse is to push for correct pricing structures allowing for network expansion through the intranetwork "loan" mechanism.

The earlier lessons concerning intertemporal commensuration are also pertinent here. With budget funds, rather than a numerical threshold value, serving as the constraint, it is probably not terribly important whether the IRR or (absolute or relative) NPV is used. In the underemployed economy framework the correct discount rate is probably higher than in the fully employed situation, and we recommend a discount rate of 4–6 percent.

For projects involving infrastructure investments as a large component (for example, problems 8.2, 8.3, or 8.4) of general tax revenues, the 4–6 percent discount rate is also appropriate. We believe this better reflects the equilibrium MPK in the LTFE economy, because even if the intertemporal social indifference curves in the fully employed and LTFE countries are the same, the consumption possibility frontiers in the latter are probably steeper at any value of present national income, that is, the gain in income tomorrow for a unit sacrifice today is assumed higher in the LTFE economy, so it will be tangent to an indifference curve at a point of steeper slope.

In addition to infrastructure projects, the public sector may have to concern itself with commercial ventures if national entrepreneurship is lacking. These investments will include both export industries and plants for domestic production, and commercial principles should thus apply. Hence, an SOE should borrow either domestically or abroad at the going rate of interest. If the gross annual cash flow can cover the amortization of interest and principal, the loan should proceed. Investment of its own internally generated funds should be optimized similarly, and if the market rate of interest is "too high," the firm should await a reduction of the rate to something more manageable, although (as in problem 6.11) direct subsidies might be considered for the industry in some situations.

Problems

8.1. The benefit and expenditure stream associated with two road designs between points A and B for each of the next ten years are shown in table 8P–1.

Table 8P–1
Calculation of Net Annual Benefit for Two Road Designs under Two Treatments of Labor Cost

Private User Benefits	Annual Maintenance		Net Benefit	
	Machinery	Labor	Traditional	Alternative Calculation
	Sophisticated Design (High paved road, deep base, wide lanes)			
500	40	10	450	
	Simple Design (Light pavement, shallow base, narrow lanes)			
240	15	60	165	

Looking just at the benefit streams, note that, as traditionally calculated, the sophisticated road benefits are 173 percent higher than the simple design benefits. If the context is an underdeveloped economy, what will be the relative benefits? Show this alternative calculation. (All machinery must be imported.)

Solution

Labor is a benefit since it represents an otherwise unused resource. Therefore it should be added rather than subtracted, giving 500 − 40 + 10 = 470 and 240 − 15 + 60 = 285, respectively, for the two designs. The difference between the benefits falls from $285,000 to $185,000, and this could easily change the ranking of the two projects. (Also see problem 6.8 for another example where it is correct to add items from opposite sides of the ledger.)

8.2. An agricultural project is designed for tender fruit production. The farms will hire unemployed workers and produce peaches and pears worth $1 million annually (at wholesale purchase prices) at the farms. Private transport costs to move the fruit to the market towns are $200,000, including $150,000 for drivers' costs at controlled minimum wages. It is believed that truck drivers' possible product in their next best opportunity would be $90,000. The drivers who will take these shipments are now unemployed. Calculate the benefit.

Solution

The $1,000,000 is a benefit, as is the drivers' labor of $150,000. The $50,000 of other vehicle costs would otherwise be utilized. Therefore, total annual benefit is $1,150,000. It is assumed that there are no other selling expenses. Also, note that the wages are counted at their market rates. They constitute a benefit to their full extent since they will be included in the final price, which reflects the desire—utility—of the fruit to final purchasers.

8.3. A small river infested with snails playing host to a tapeworm has discouraged local agriculture. The river can be cleared of snails for an initial cost of $5,000,000 and an annual supplementary purification of $1,000,000. The land is well suited for cotton.

There are very few people in the area today—no more than a hundred or so. But there have been persistent recurring droughts up north, and there is reason to believe about 5,000 families will move to the area if the river can be cleared. Each family would grow $800 worth of cotton, using family labor, and $200 worth of chemical fertilizer provided on credit. In addition, each family will grow $300 worth of food crops for its own consumption.

Finally, although families will bring their personal possessions, they will leave behind their modest housing. However, they can build adobe (mud) beehive huts in the new region. These will take about three months effort by husband and wife and will last six years before becoming uninhabitable. The type of labor expended on construction is elsewhere paid $2 per day and comparable quality housing in nearby towns rents for $90 per year.

The potential migrants had been earning about $400 per family in agriculture (including subsistence cultivation). In the last four drought years, however, their earnings fell to $250, and the region has become so devastated that there is little expectation of return to earlier conditions.

Calculate the benefits.

Solution

Cotton production: 5000 × 800	+4,000,000
Less fertilizer: 5000 × 200	−1,000,000
Plus subsistence production: 5000 × 300	+1,500,000
Plus imputed rent value of home: 5000 × 90	+ 450,000
Less forgone earnings: 5000 × 250	−1,250,000
Less annual river maintenance	−1,000,000
Less housing depreciation	− 250,000
Total	$2,500,000

In addition we must add the value of construction (5000 × $2 × 2 persons × 25 days × 3 months = $1,500,000).

8.4. Economists in Ecalpon are evaluating an irrigation project for a potentially fertile valley where annual subsistence farming today produces $250,000 of crops per year, but which, following irrigation, will produce $1,000,000 annually (cash value of crops paid to farmers). The basis for valuing the crops is the same throughout. Today Ecalpon is very underdeveloped, although it has some medium scale industry which it is trying to promote. For example, its metal products industry is capable of producing medium and small diameter metal pipe and forming seamless vinyl pipe from stock, but it is unlikely to undertake production of vehicles, fuel, or petrochemicals for the next thirty years, the local market simply being too small with little chance of exports.

The project will take one year to build (year zero), employing $3,000,000 worth of local labor (half of which would otherwise be idle). Agricultural operations will proceed at full speed during the year immediately following. Machinery worth $1,000,000 will be totally used up in the construction and there will also be materials inputs of $1,400,000 from the fully employed sector of the economy.

You are given the following data (all estimates have been carefully prepared) to calculate the annual net benefits for year zero and the first ten years of operation. Do this and enter the results B_t, C_t, and $B_t - C_t$ in a table.

Table 8P-2
Effects of Irrigation Project (First Ten Years of Operation)

Annual Agricultural Production		$1,000,000
Annual Inputs of Fertilizer		
Purchase Price	$150,000	
Import Duty	50,000	
Subtotal		170,000

Table 8P-2 (continued)

Annual Transportation Cost to Market the Production[a]		
Fuel	50,000	
Depreciation of Vehicles	50,000	
Wages	200,000	
Subtotal		300,000
Annual Maintenance of Irrigation Works by Unskilled Local Labor		
Wages	50,000	
Small Implements (Shovels, and so on)	5,000	
Subtotal		55,000
Replace Network of Final Distribution Pipework by Unskilled Local Labor, Every Five Years		
Wages	25,000	
Pipe (Imported) Purchase Price	50,000	
Customes Duty	10,000	
Subtotal		85,000

[a]The purchase price of the vehicle to the truck driver includes a 25 percent duty. Depreciation is calculated on a straight line basis, that is, purchase price divided by number of years of operation. This pattern correctly measures physical wear. There are no import duties on fuel.

Solution

Table 8P-3
Calculation of Annual Benefits, Costs, and Net Benefits of Irrigated Project

Year	Item	Gross Benefit	Cost	Net Benefit
0[a]		1,500,000	3,900,000	−2,400,000
1–4 and 6–9	Additional Agricultural Production	750,000	—	
	Fertilizer[b]	—	150,000	
	Fuel [c]	—	50,000	
	Depreciation[d]	—	40,000	
	Drivers' Wages	200,000	—	
	Irrigation Maintenance			
	Wages	50,000		
	Materials[e]	5,000		
	Total	1,005,000	240,000	765,000
5 and 10	Network Replacement			
	Wages	25,000	—	
	Pipe[f]	—	60,000	
	Total	25,000	60,000	−35,000

Table 8P-3 (continued)

[a] Employment of idle labor ($1,500,000) is a benefit. Machinery, intermediate inputs, and diverted labor are costs.

[b] Duty not a cost since there is no possibility that petrochemicals production will be undertaken.

[c] Since there is no duty, no tariff adjustment need even be considered.

[d] The import duty is not a protective tariff. It is not a cost.

[e] Small scale industry assumed to expand to provide this need.

[f] There is a national industry capable of producing pipe. Duty is protective and imports then run counter to policy and constitute a cost.

9
Consumer Surplus

Consumer surplus continues to be advocated by many writers for use in project evaluation. While it may be valid for certain restricted conditions, we believe there are several weaknesses which vitiate its general use. There are two types: inconsistencies in application and measurement; inconsistencies in theory. The first should be looked at by anyone involved in project evaluation who may be tempted to try this method; the theoretic problems require a more extended study and could, without loss, be deferred on a first reading. Accordingly, they are placed in an appendix to this chapter.

Historical Background

The concept of consumer surplus was devised in the mid-nineteenth century by a French civil engineer, Jules Dupuit, who was trying to formulate a criterion for deciding whether or not to build a bridge. Hypothesizing a downward sloping demand curve, he called the area under the curve the "absolute utility." He called the difference between it and the annual cost of maintenance (plus the interest on capital expended in construction) "the relative utility" (Dupuit 1968, 38). In this passage Dupuit neglects the construction expenditure itself, and it is not clear whether or not he intended it to be included with interest as a blended amortization payment, although in the immediately following paragraph he set the goal of producing "the greatest possible utility and at the same time a *revenue to cover the cost of upkeep and interest on capital*" (emphasis added). Note that this conflicts with the modern interpretation of public-sector norms, which forswears collection of interest payments for such an undertaking on the ground that they represent not a real marginal cost (that is, resource cost), but merely an expense; moreover, in the Dupuit case, which was a footbridge, even upkeep is independent of use and strictly a function of time—again not an output-variable, traffic-variable cost and, hence, not appropriate for recovery.

However, the concept has come to be associated primarily with Alfred Marshall's name, because of the development and careful critical scrutiny to which he subjected it in his *Principles*. Interestingly, one main difference between Dupuit's treatment and Marshall's is the location of the apostrophe: although Dupuit did not actually use the expression, he was talking about the surplus that would arise on behalf of *many* consumers, whereas most of Marshall's treatment concerned the welfare measurement for an *individual* consumer. In fact, his recognition of the obstacle—declining marginal utility of money—to using the concept for even a single consumer, plus the further recognition that this same obstacle would preclude aggregation over individuals at different income levels, restrained him from advocating the approach as a general analytical tool. There is a curious irony here: many writers believe he was a strong supporter of this concept and now—after years of critical examinaton in which it has been rejected, reworked, rehabilitated, accepted by some, and still rejected by others—refer to the concept that Marshall never accepted as the "Marshallian consumer surplus."

Inconsistencies in Application

Many writers on project evaluation advocate consumer surplus as the correct project decision criterion. Although others disagree, there seems to be little discussion of it today—the two groups almost talking past one another, rather than reinvestigating the issue with the intention of finally resolving it. Perhaps the concept is not questioned more often because it appears to be successfully employed in practice—project decisions are often based on comparisons between the discounted flow of annual consumer surpluses and the investment expenditure. However, we should not call applications successful merely because they reach answers which may in fact be far from socially optimal; rather the relevance of the tool itself to the particular situation should be penetratingly questioned. Even in situations when reality corresponds more or less to the main assumption of the theory—constant marginal utility of money for individuals and groups of individuals—too often the consistency of the available data with the requirements of the theory cannot be taken for granted, and/or other untenable assumptions are introduced. (Marginal utility of money, today's terminology, was called by Marshall "marginal degree of utility." See appendix 9A.) It is best to illustrate this view through a series of examples. In the first two we assume constant marginal utility of money for each person and between persons. In these cases the relation between measured benefit and social welfare will be insensitive to distribution.

Neglect of Private-Sector Consumer Surplus

While consumer surplus is advocated for use in the public sector, it is never advocated for private-sector investments. Its omission will clearly bias investment toward the public sector and reduce economic efficiency. This procedure is usually justified on the ground that a private-sector investment—in steel, say—will generate an output used as an intermediate good for countless products each of which is associated with a trivial triangle even though the demand curve for each is downward sloping (Problem 9.1). Therefore, it should be neglected; but if the outputs reflect increased consumption of the present population, no matter how small the triangles, they should be summed up and credited to the investment if we are to use consumer surplus. Nobody, as far as I know, proposed that we do this. Of course, even within the public sector this practice also biases investment in favor of activities such as transport or power production, rather than traditional industrial activities such as appliance or raw materials production.

Improper Treatment of Radically Different Technologies

Now assume the investment is to be made in a project embodying a technology radically different from the present one. The characteristics of the services rendered by each may be identical, at one extreme, or very different. For concreteness, imagine a bridge over water now crossed by ferry or small boat. We know present traffic, and assume that somehow we know with certainty what traffic will be once the bridge is built. (It may be asked why, if the services are identical, the bridge is not already in place. The answer might be that when travel began there were not enough users to justify the bridge, but, as time passed, density grew enough to stimulate contemplation of the bridge. In addition, construction costs may have fallen due to engineering advances.)

If the services rendered are identical, there is a single indifference map for crossings (versus all other consumption). The consumer assigns no value or onus to such factors as scenery, time, reaction to prolonged exposure to water, seasickness, and so on. We could, in principle, recover the single demand curve from a single indifference map, and we could calculate a meaningful consumer surplus measure. The consumer surplus approach *is* reasonable in this type of situation, which we believe is implicitly assumed by advocates of consumer surplus, especially those employing a bridge as illustration (for example, Bergson, Harberger in recent writings). The problem of comparing this benefit to one elsewhere, which is measured in rectangular terms (for example, profit, cost reduction, or, in a situation of high unemployment, national income generation), would still have to be resolved. It may seem unreasonable to assume similar services—especially with regard to crossing time—but the possibility must be allowed. Even if there are differences in crossing time and other factors which appear to be more substantial (but not so as to cause a radical reorganization of the basic economy) and which would preclude the hypothesis of a single demand curve, this approach is reasonable. There is some evidence that this would be a fairly good characterization of the potential fixed link (bridge, tunnel, or combination) across the Strait of Georgia between Vancouver Island and the lower mainland of British Columbia, for example.

But if the services are so different in terms of their ancillary characteristics as to introduce a radical change in consumption patterns for large numbers of people (for example, the shift in residential patterns with their very different commuter patterns, or creation of new long-distance travel patterns—both of which occurred after the construction of the Verrazano–Narrows Bridge across the entrance to New York harbor), we can no longer regard the activity levels as points on a single demand curve, but, rather, as points on two different curves. We must construct (how?) the demand curves for ferry and bridge crossings. Then we subtract the consumer surplus triangle now being realized under the present pattern (A) from the surplus under the bridge use pattern (B) (figure 9–1).

Unequal Utility of Income Among Consumers

So far we have assumed constant marginal utility of income within and between consumers. But this assumption—especially the between-consumer part of it, which would require constancy at widely different income levels—is clearly wrong, as Marshall himself repeatedly emphasized (see

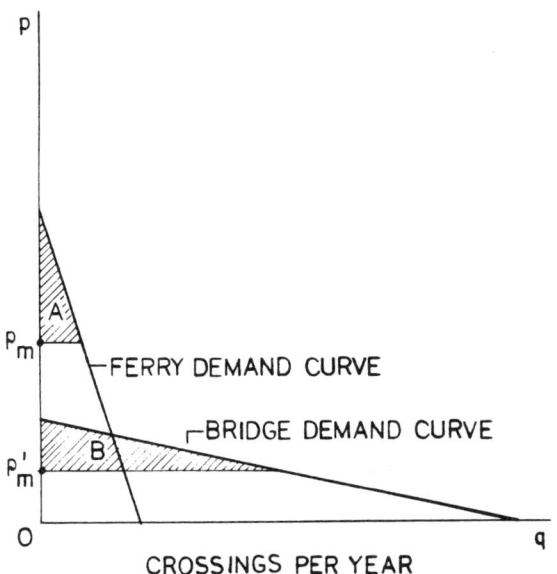

Figure 9–1. Calculation of Change in Consumer Surplus from Bridge Investment

appendix to this chapter). Nevertheless, many people argue that consumer surplus should serve as the main organizing analytical device: if it is flawed, so is national income. Three sorts of arguments are given to support this view: (1) decreasing marginal utility of money also distorts national income comparisons; (2) consumer surplus is not intended to be taken literally, but should be construed to reflect *any* gains over market prices; and (3) consumer surplus can be adjusted by distributional weights to determine the social valuation of individuals' marginal utilities. Let us examine these arguments.

1. First, the alleged unreasonableness of denying the validity of consumer surplus on the ground that the marginal utility of income is not constant, while yet accepting changes in national income as reflections of welfare change: if the marginal utility of income is decreasing, it is argued, surely a $1,000 change will be associated with different utilities at regional income levels of $1,000,000 and $10,000,000.

This is a valid assertion. However, the methodology we are propounding does not require otherwise: the rectangular criteria we have advocated, which originate in and are consistent with the use of national income as a criterion, are to be compared to one another at a given income level. At a regional income of $1,000,000,000 say, it *is* reasonable to compare two projects whose national income generation may differ, but which both are small in relation to present income—for example, projects with a net benefit of $1,000,000 or $1,500,000. Moreover, because of our recommended treatment for inputs and resources newly absorbed into the production process, projects which affect secular unemployment in otherwise unpriced, intermediate good production are more attractive in national income terms (recall problem 8.1). This is proper, since they make a greater contribution in terms of utility (Problem 9.2).

2. What about the second criticism?

It may be argued that consumer surplus was never intended to be taken literally. Each point on the aggregate market demand curve represents the price that someone is willing to pay for the next unit of consumption. Thus, each person is permitted a unique demand function, and the aggregate market demand curve merely sums their graphs horizontally. Each person's valuation at any quantity x is given by the price at that quantity, $p(x)$, and reflects *his* estimation of the convenience, time saving, attractiveness, reduced expenses on other goods or services, and so on. If the consumer is then asked to pay something less than this, his net gain from consumption of *that* unit in each period is given by the difference between $p(x)$ and p_m, the market price he is actually asked to pay.

The situation just examined should not be confused with consumer surplus. We stress that inclusion of such benefits, to the extent that they can be isolated, is indeed one of the principles in our national accounting framework: we should value time or other conveniences if they can be inferred, and we have repeatedly stressed the need to make imputations to take account of such benefits. If potential users of a facility can each save twenty minutes, a rectangular measure of their benefit—equal to 20(unit value) − 20(p_m)—should be added to the other project benefits. However, a confident feeling in our estimates of group size and unit value implies that we can isolate these benefits and beneficiaries if we try; then we can impose a unit charge which is practically equal to the unit net benefit. We could, and should, discriminate by user class, time of day, multiplicity of use, and so on. This restrains the indiscriminate and inefficient overinvestment to which the public sector may be prone, and since we usually should emplace a collection mechanism for the output-variable costs in any event, only a small amount of collection cost will be added.

3. Finally, what can be said about distributional weights to overcome the increasing maldistribution following the use of consumer surplus?

It has frequently been argued that the problem could be skirted by applying income adjustments to each dollar of measured benefit. The marginal tax rate (MTR) represents a proper adjustment mechanism under certain conditions (basically that 1-MTR does represent society's valuation of the marginal utility to each consumer under a reasonably responsible and honest tax collection effort). These conditions are realistically hard to achieve in fact, although if we knew that they held, the consumer surplus criterion with distribution weights could be a reasonable approach. However—given the problems in determining welfare through consumer surplus as shown in previous examples—even if dollars could be adjusted to provide a standard utility measure, projects with benefits evaluated through consumer surplus would still have an artificially induced edge over projects which did not. Since, moreover, there is uncertainty about precisely what the tax rates do reflect and about the effectiveness of tax enforcement, it is better to use a consistent approach to benefit measurement, such as the national income framework.

Appendix 9A
Marshall, Consumer Surplus, and the Marginal Utility of Money

The major theoretic objections to Marshall's consumer surplus measure are those which follow from the unreasonable assumption and implications of constant marginal utility of money, which is required for the measure to be meaningful. Samuelson showed in his *Foundations of Economic Analysis* that constancy must refer to something like real income rather than nominal income, and he then demonstrated that it would imply unitary price elasticity of demand for any commodity, a relation that simply does not hold in real markets. Although we recognize that this violation of reality compromises the constancy assumption, it is often argued that marginal utility is approximately constant for small changes in income and the zero income effect following a price fall (which logically requires that assumption) is approximately correct much of the time. Therefore, the implied constancy, and with it the consumer surplus measure of welfare gain, can be accepted after all.

In this appendix I will argue that: Marshall did not hold and did not need the assumption of constant marginal utility of money (as that concept is now understood); and consumer surplus is not a good measure of welfare gain. Moreover, I suspect that Marshall would agree with this criticism on empirical grounds.

In order that the "Marshallian consumer surplus"—the area under the market demand curve between prices p_1 and p_2—be an acceptable measure of the social welfare change accompanying the price change, the marginal utility of money (income) must be constant. This is necessary for two reasons:

1. To compare his own welfare before and after changes in price and consumption, each individual consumer must have an unvarying measure denominated in a fixed unit, the utility of one extra dollar.

2. The market demand curve is the horizontal sum of the individual demand curves. If the area under the curve is to be a meaningful measure of welfare change, the utility of each dollar of difference between the demand price for any inframarginal unit of consumption and the equilibrium market price must be the same for any two individuals. Since their incomes may be very different, this can be the case only if the utility of each extra dollar is constant for all levels of income (that is, if the marginal utility of money is constant).

Now, the notion of constant marginal utility of money conflicts with our basic postulate that the utility of any commodity increases at a decreasing rate as the volume of that commodity increases—that is, the marginal utility is decreasing. Accordingly, some authors fault Marshall for holding this unreasonable assumption (and its implied zero income effect on consumption of a good following a price change), and then argue that, in the particular example at hand, marginal utility does not decrease very much and the income effect is small so that the measuring rod is virtually constant and there is no possibility of double counting. Frequent appeals for support are made to a well-known passage from Hicks.[a]

The truth is that Marshall did *not* accept the constancy hypothesis, either for an individual or for consumers at different income levels. Since this conflicts with the usual view of things, I would like to offer the following citations testifying to this view—but first some differences in the terminology, which have drawn too little attention, should be mentioned. (All references are to the eighth edition of Marshall's *Principles of Economics*.)

Marshall employed three terms to mean two different things: on the one hand he uses "marginal value of money" (p. 109) and "marginal degree of utility of money" (p. 691) to mean what we call "marginal utility of money." ("If m is the amount of money or general purchasing power at a person's disposal at any time, and μ represents its total utility to him, then $d\mu/dm$ represents the marginal degree of utility to him." [p. 690]). On the other hand, "If u be the total utility of an amount x of a commodity to a given person at a given time, then marginal utility is measured by $(du/dx)\delta x$" (ibid.). Thus, Marshall's marginal utility of money is the marginal degree of utility of money multiplied by a differential; but, since marginal degree of utility (our marginal utility) *is assumed* to be decreasing, the only way a situation in which money is an unchanged measuring rod can eventuate is if the amount of money at the consumer's disposal does not change. That is, the differential in income resulting from the price change must be zero, implying that the amount spent on the commodity following the price change must be unchanged. In other words, *its price elasticity must be unitary*, a characteristic which is not believed to be true in general. The point is, however, that Marshall, though not working in terms of elasticity, believed the equivalent hypothesis of zero income differential to be unsound.

We have so far focused on the implications of constancy and noncon-

---

[a] "What in the light of this approach, we have been trying to do is to establish more precisely than Marshall thought necessary, the conditions needed for the Marshall measure to be a good measure. And, so considered, the result of our inquiry is very simple. In order that the Marshall measure of consumer's surplus should be a good measure, one thing alone is needful—that the income effect should be small." We note that when objecting to the Marshallian measure and offering his other consumer surpluses, Hicks stressed that each answered a different question and, though none could be assumed to be the main question of interest, the compensating variation and the compensated demand curve have come to be accepted as the main alternatives to the Marshallian approach.

stancy for the individual consumer and the use of the Marshallian triangle to infer changes in the consumer's welfare (even though Marshall sometimes placed the apostrophe after the "s"). Now, what can be said about constancy and the whole community?

Marshall made numerous qualifications concerning behavior of consumers—that the middle-income or rich individual may have different tastes, and so on. Thus, the marginal utility of twopence is recognized to be different for a rich man and a poor man (p. 81): "the richer a man becomes the less is the marginal utility of money to him" (p. 81); demand schedules are presented for rich, middle class, and poor consumers (p. 88); a "pound's worth of satisfaction to an ordinary poor man is a much greater thing than a pound's worth of satisfaction to an ordinary rich man" (p. 108); "the marginal utility of a thing to anyone diminishes with every increase in the amount of it he already has" (p. 79). The importance of this nonconstancy for the interpretation of the community's surplus is that the area under the market demand curve does not, in general, measure the welfare change for the community. This point was explicitly and emphatically recognized by Marshall, but it has been given negligible attention, while the acceptance of the assumption of virtual constancy under a price change for the individual consumer has often been taken as equivalent to constancy between consumers or for any one individual at widely different income levels. On the other hand, a situation might arise in which the market demand curve and the related Marshallian surplus would be acceptable to measure welfare change. If so, it can be used to guide decisions. We should be careful, though, not to treat the exception as the rule; the fact that such a situation is possible does not mean that the method is generally valid. Marshall recognized this; thus, if by "Marshallian" we mean someone who holds the view that the area under the market demand curve between p_1 and p_2 represents the welfare gain resulting from the price change, we would have to conclude that Marshall was not a Marshallian.

Problems

9.1. 1. A new steel production process could reduce production costs for steel, now imported, by $30 per ton. After processing into sheet, shapes, extrusions, and other parts, this would translate into retail price reductions of $20, $18, $15, and $75 for stoves, refrigerators, washing machines, and automobiles, respectively. The corresponding demand curves over a wide price range are linear:

$$q_{01} = 2{,}000 - 100\, p_{01};$$
$$q_{02} = 1{,}900 - 80\, p_{02};$$
$$q_{03} = 1{,}800 - 150\, p_{03};$$
$$q_{03} = 2{,}000 - 300\, p_{04};$$

148 • *Project Decision Making in the Public Sector*

Determine the total consumer surplus. (Today's prices are $600, $700, $400, and $5000.)

2. The retail price reductions reflect in part the replacement of certain other materials by steel (some aluminum and plastic parts). How does this affect your calculation in the first part?

Solution

1. First, present consumption of the four appliances is: 1,940,000; 1,844,000; 1,740,000; and 500,000, respectively. Then the calculations in table 9–1 may be made.

Table 9–1
Consumer Surplus and Simple Cost Reduction Calculations for Four Consumer Durables

New Price p_{1i}	New Quantity q_{1i}	CS = $\frac{1}{2}(q_0 + q_1)$ $(p_0 - p_1)$	Cost Reduction $q_0(p_0 - p_1)$	CS − CR
580	1,942,000	38,820,000	38,800,000	20,000
682	1,845,440	33,204,960	33,192,000	12,960
385	1,742,250	26,116,875	26,100,000	16,875
4925	522,500	38,343,750	37,500,000	843,750
Total		136,485,585	135,592,000	893,585

The difference made by the CS criterion is small in relation to total cost reduction. Nevertheless, it must be considered if we wish to use a CS approach. (Note: It is usually not large if CS is correctly calculated for infrastructure projects either.)

2. As long as demand curves slope downward, which follows from basic assumptions of economic rationality, some CS must be forgone in the substitution of steel for these other products, but it would not be possible to trace through all impacts on prices, wages, and incomes.

9.2. Suppose there is just enough left in the budget to choose between two projects:

a. the low-grade road in problem 8.1, and
b. a caviar processing plant which will reduce caviar costs at the consumer level by $205,000 annually but will generate CS, calculated through the ordinary market demand curve, of $285,000.

Some people are pushing for the plant, whose annual benefit exceeds the road benefit (traditional calculation) by $120,000. Against them is a group invoking Marshall with his continual references to the declining marginal utility of income, couched in arguments such as those on page 147. A third group points out that, in any event, national income figures do not distinguish income or expenditures by recipient. What would you suggest?

Solution

If we wish to use consumer surplus, we must be consistent. The consumer surplus of the simple design road will then be at least equal to the consumer surplus implicit in the consumption of a dollar volume equal to the user cost savings of $225,000 plus the surplus associated with the generation of income of $60,000 in the hands of people who are undoubtedly poorer than the caviar consumers. Thus, the total CS of the road project will be at least $285,000, while the CS of the caviar project is just equal to $285,000, implying that the road should be selected. If, alternatively, the national income criterion is used, the benefits of the projects are equal to $285,000 for the road and $205,000 in cost savings for caviar production.

Bibliographic Note

The original paper by Dupuit, cited in the bibliograhic note to chapter 1, was published in 1844. To this are traced both the genesis of consumer surplus and the intellectual kernel of marginal cost pricing, although, as we have pointed out, Dupuit did not disavow the objective of collecting tolls to cover interest, time-variable maintenance, or interest on the bonds. In a 1976 paper we argue that the bridges Dupuit spent most of his time talking about were footbridges, for which the concept of marginal cost and resolution of the long-run versus short-run dilemma is particularly simple, there being only one design that could reasonably be considered. (Marshall's treatment depended on here is that of the eighth edition of his *Principles*.) Hicks's criticisms were presented in several papers in the early 1940s, and his widely quoted reconciliation is contained in *A Revision of Demand Theory,* while unrepentant Samuelson's objections are contained in his *Foundations*. The paper by Currie, Murphy, and Schmitz cited in the bibliographic note to chapter 6 was the most complete survey of the field up to the time of its writing. The more recent papers by Bergson and Harberger favor use of consumer surplus, with bridges coincidentally, as the prototype project. There has also been a resurgence of interest in the conditions under which consumer surplus provides an accurate measure of welfare change for the individual consumer during the last five to eight years, with many papers on the subject appearing in the *American Economic Review*. However, most of these implicitly or explicitly assume a stable indifference map for the consumer with price changes for just one product. Generalizing to even a single customer with dynamic interdependencies in demand (for example, for someone who moves to Staten Island following the bridge construction), let alone to a whole community, requires extreme caution.

References

Abouchar, Alan. "Dupuit's Bridges and the Theory of Marginal Cost Pricing," *History of Political Economy* Vol. 8, no. 2 (1976).

Bergson, Abram. "Note on Consumer's Surplus," *Journal of Economic Literature* Vol XIII, no. 1 (March 1975).

Harberger, A.C. "Three Basic Postulates for Applied Welfare Economics: An Interpretive Essay." *Journal of Economic Literature* vol. IX, no. 3 (September 1971).

Hicks, John. *A Revision of Demand Theory.* Oxford: Clarendon Press, 1956.

Marshall, Alfred. *Principles of Economics.* 8th ed. (1926). London: Macmillan, 1956.

Samuelson, Paul. *Foundations of Economic Analysis.* Cambridge: Harvard University Press, 1947.

10
Taking Account of Inflation

We must distinguish between two kinds of inflation: generalized inflation in which all sectors of the economy undergo equal or approximately equal rates of price change, and differential inflation in which, while the overall price level is rising, the rates of increase differ markedly between sectors. Between the end of World War II and the mid-1960s there was little of either kind in most modern industrialized economies, but annual rates of 2–3 percent began to be experienced subsequently.

Then sharp increases in oil prices set off energy and related sector inflation, reinforced by the legacy of the Vietnam war, and quickly reverberated through the economy, leading to annual inflation rates of up to 15 percent or more in industrialized countries. In the Third World, generalized inflation of much higher rates, ranging up to 200 percent and more annually, has a much longer tradition, and in these countries differential inflation is also significant today, with the energy sector leading the price increases.

In this chapter we look at the most important aspects of inflation for project evaluation. Our conclusions are that as long as generalized, rather than differential, inflation is at issue, the future benefit and cost time streams may be estimated on the basis of present-day values and discounted by the real social rate of discount. What is absolutely essential, however, is to revalue the capital input, at least once a year, in order to set product prices correctly and avoid incorrect market signals to planners of future projects. This certainly relates to variable capital expenditures undertaken as part of the initial investment expense, but it also relates to the isochronic costs, to the extent that repeated investments in similar projects may be expected—subway extensions, sequential river crossings, community tennis courts, and so on. For differential inflation the problem is somewhat more complicated, and it is preferable to measure the time stream of benefits by the prices expected to be relevant to each year in the stream.

Generalized Inflation

If there is generalized inflation at a constant annual rate r, the nominal returns in year t will exceed real returns by a factor $(1 + r)^t - 1$. In this case we may use either the real returns and real social rate of discount d or nominal returns and "nominal" social discount rate $(1 + d)(1 + r) - 1$. Since projecting inflation is difficult, the use of nominal rates and projected inflation may simply introduce distortions. Therefore the use of real magnitudes is preferable.

There are two exceptions to the proposed approach: projects financed by revenue bonds and SOE activities. We first consider SOE activities.

State-Owned Enterprises

Industrial firms are increasingly aware of the need to take inflation into account when evaluating their performance through accounts which reflect fixed capital replacement values and price changes for materials and inventories. The use of such an accounting is primarily retrospective—to analyze the recent real performance of a firm in order to make an inference about the future outlook.

The SOE also must borrow money at the market rate of interest (with no preference, one hopes). Therefore, the payback of a socially efficient investment can be assured only if the annual cash flow covers the annual interest and depreciation payments, which may be higher because the market interest is higher in anticipation of continued inflation. Clearly, then, the cash flow must be calculated at the nominal, that is, inflated, future prices. Since we are assuming general inflation, the broadest inflation measure—the GNE or GNP implicit price deflator—should be forecast to adjust the future revenue stream to reflect this continuing inflation.

Revenue Bond Financing

For revenue bonds much the same reasoning applies. If we *can* assume that revenue bond financing leads to efficient outcomes (recall the qualifications concerning the possibility of higher-level bailouts and federal tax exclusion, both of which may influence investors' opinions of private returns and the analyst's view of the social efficiency of the projects), the bond will have to be repaid out of current revenues. Since, with inflation, the rate of interest will be higher than it would otherwise be by a factor equal to the rate of inflation, the inflated revenues will have to cover payments. These revenues are the relevant consideration in this case. Physical output should, therefore, be valued at the future prices reflecting this inflation.

Differential Inflation

The price level in individual sectors or regions may change faster or slower than the average price level (problem 10.1). Ready examples of differential sectoral price movement are fuel prices, which, having risen in export countries by around 2,000 percent since 1973, are reflected in retail gasoline prices which rose by 50 percent in relation to the average price level in the United States in the 1970s (the price increases are somewhat muted by the existence of price restrictions in the United States on "old oil"—oil whose reserves were established earlier). Third World non-oil-producing countries saw much higher real increases in energy prices than the United States did.

Examples of regionally differentiated price movements are the grain price movements that may accompany intensification of regional development, or even motor vehicle operating costs in a rapidly growing area as compared to average transport costs. Thus, a road versus rail decision in a high-growth region should take account of the differential operating cost movements in the future as the transport artery becomes crowded.

Whenever differential price movements can be anticipated, they should be used to value both inputs and outputs. The essential justification for this is that the price relationships in any year are the best measure of the relative value of an input or output in that year, and to say that the price of one good rises in relation to the other means that the first good becomes relatively more useful to society. The distinction between goods or factors may be their location or their essential nature—blue-collar workers versus office staff or highly skilled production workers, flour versus eggs, movies versus beef. Whenever there is a suspicion that secular price movements are taking place or can be expected in the future, they must be taken into account.

Revenue Bond Financing

Here recall that we must depend on private investors' willingness to invest directly in a public-sector project and in their assessment of the project's ability to generate enough revenue—by creating enough benefits —to repay the bonds. This revenue will be subject to fluctuations in nominal terms, but, under differential inflation, this may often also reflect fluctuations in real terms. For example, a bridge built as a ferry substitute will continue to generate time savings, but the value that motorists ascribe to these savings will depend partly on the evolution of prices for other consumption. Thus, if vehicle production costs or fuel costs rise, the amount a motorist will willingly spend for time savings on a trip will fall and so will revenue as will the authority's ability to repay the bonds. Obviously, possible changes in administration and maintenance costs for the facility must also be examined. Thus, it is not so much a question of deflating future benefits to put them in real terms, but of projecting price movements to determine whether the cash flow—revenues less annual expenditures on operations and maintenance—is enough to repay the bonds and interest.

State-Owned Enterprises

SOEs, in our view, are constrained to behave as private corporations, maximizing profits, and subject to regulatory constraint if they are near-monopolies and to specific subsidies for income distribution-related or national-political objectives. This will require careful analysis of the future trends in selling prices and production costs associated with any particular investment project to determine whether revenue, less incremental costs, exceeds amortization and interest on the investment. One aspect of special importance is the life assumed for the assets, which clearly should correspond as closely as possible to the expected economic life, although this life itself may depend on the behavior of other prices.

At the very least, the difference between the nominal revenue and cost magnitudes (looking just at inputs other than those purchased as part of the investment) must cover the loan repayment and interest (or capital depreciation if bought with own funds). However, since these essentially reflect original purchase price rather than replacement costs, projected nominal current cash flow should be compared against depreciation figured against replacement value as well. Indeed, if the corporation is a quasi-monopoly, as is often the case, special care should be taken to ensure that product prices are based on replacement-cost depreciation in order to guard against overstimulation of demand and the apparent need to reinvest in socially inefficient projects in the future. Otherwise, the problem—rife in many economies—of charging a rapidly dwindling price for current consumption of capital assets employed in production will exaggerate the apparent attractiveness of this type of activity and falsely encourage the firm to reinvest. This cannot be discouraged simply by requiring positive and maximum profits for the firm, unless its costs are based on capital asset replacement costs rather than original acquisition prices. It frequently happens, however, that demand is inefficiently encouraged by firms, which then must continue to provide capacity for the demand which has evolved even though the cost of doing so exceeds the benefit. Being a financially constrained SOE may not be sufficient protection against this behavior, so we reemphasize it here (problems 10.2 and 10.3).

Problems

10.1. 1. In Ecalpon five commodity groups are consumed—foods, clothing, appliances, housing, and fuel. The respective price indexes behaved as follows since 1973 (1973 = 100). Only two years are shown.

	$I_{fo} = I_1$	$I_c = I_2$	$I_a = I_3$	$I_h = I_4$	$I_{fu} = I_5$
1974	100	100	100	100	110
1983	165	160	170	190	240

Calculate the overall price index for 1974 and 1983 if the component indexes are weighted equally.

2. Suppose, instead, that each subindex in 1983 stood at 185. How might this have come about?

Solution

1. 102; 185.

2. Probably through simple money creation.

10.2. When Ecalpon Hydro was established twenty-five years ago, it provided electricity to Chieftown on a full-cost recovery basis. When inflation accelerated, however, the combination of lethargy and misunderstood economic principles concerning sunk costs and public goods combined to hold rates down to their original levels. Some economists are now pressing for pricing based on replacement cost in order to eliminate the inefficiency which this has caused.
1. What form may this inefficiency be taking, that is, in what form is it being manifested?
2. How would you propose to deal with this problem?

Solution

1. This pricing policy may have any or all of the following consequences:
    a. Induce migration to the city inefficiently since energy is being priced below its price elsewhere. Note, migration by itself is not evidence of inefficiency, but it may be causing inefficient congestion by overburdening the lines and causing supply disruptions; or it may simply be causing congestion in the city but not disrupting power supply—overstraining sewer facilities, traffic, and so on. Recalling the congestion analysis of chapter 4, however—difficult enough on a simple single highway—discourages the hope of easily determining this congestion cost, but we do know that if people are rational and price distortions exist, there will be some inefficiency.
    b. Encourage business to establish here, thus inducing migration, which may be inefficient;
    c. After the foregoing influences have been exerted for a few years, lead the city to subsidize further electric power capacity, it being too difficult politically to adjust prices to a real incremental social cost basis which would take into account the higher costs of new capacity.

156 • *Project Decision Making in the Public Sector*

    2. Revalue capacity at replacement cost and include a depreciation component in the power price. Price discrimination should be pursued to recover the joint costs, with prices for the joint components directly related to demand intensity, as shown in chapter 3.

10.3. As it turned out, the proponents of replacement-cost pricing won out, and it was decided to depreciate all fixed capital on the basis of what it would cost to replace existing equipment and installations with new facilities (suitable allowance being made for technological changes and degree of wear). Depreciation would henceforth be calculated on this basis. An opportunity cost school feels a little uncomfortable with this new view, however, at least as far as the isochronic elements are concerned. They argue, moreover, that inefficiency alleged to exist cannot be proven but only logically deduced.

It is also possible to reach an alternative conclusion and some economists argue that the electric facilities are part of the social infrastructure and should be provided as a public good anyway (that is, with little or no attempt to recover costs), with the heavy demand vindicating their view. They also assert that thermal station no. 1, which is one of Ecalpon Hydro's plants, but is not interconnected with the system, is operating in a southwestern region which is in a secular downturn, and raising the price by introducing replacement-cost pricing would only exacerbate the decline, since even fewer industries would be attracted to the region. How would you reconcile the opposing positions?

Solution

The concept of opportunity cost, correctly applied, leads to policies which seem at a superficial level to be diametrically opposed, although they are fully compatible when the concept is correctly understood. Here, it calls for valuing and depreciating the power capacity for Chieftown at replacement cost and valuing thermal station no. 1 at any price at all down to zero.

    Opportunity cost tells us that the value of the factor is determined by the value it can produce. Sometimes, however, we do not have information on all the specific values being produced, and we must be guided by what people would be willing to pay for it on the reasonable assumption that they would not be willing to pay more than the value they derive from it. This must be compared to the deterioration of value caused over the year by the use of the facility. This deterioration will be the difference between the value of the facility at the start and at the end of the year *if the facility is to be replaced*. If the city is thriving, as is Chieftown, the facility will have to be replaced one day. Therefore, replacement cost is the appropriate basis for valuation and depreciation, even according to the opportunity cost view. However, since thermal station no. 1 is located in a decaying region, it will probably not need to be replaced, so its use causes no one any loss since it does not hasten the day of replacement by causing the plant to wear out. It also does not artificially and inefficiently induce demand. Note, however, that if there is enough demand so that the equilibrium demand price, determined by the existing capacity, exceeds the further incremental cost (short-run marginal cost in the usual terminology), something will have to be charged as a rationing device, but this amount need have no relation at all to either original purchase price or replacement cost.

Index

Aaa bonds, 52. *See also* Moody's
AASHO coefficient, 37–38, 117
AASHO road test, 18, 39
Abouchar, Alan, 10, 43, 150
Absolute net present value, 84
Acquisition cost. *See* Historic cost
Agriculture, 41, 103–107, 134–137
Airport traffic, 4, 5
Alchian, A.A., 91
Allocatively inefficient demand. *See* Socially efficient demand
Amortization, 15, 36, 89–91
Anoprosthetic demand, 22, 29, 33
Anticipated consumption frontier, 80, 113
Appalachia, 97
ASC. *See* Average social cost
Average social cost, 56, 119–121

Beesley, M.E., 59
Belem–Brasilia highway, 116
Benefit measurement, 93–107
Bergmann, Barbara, 107
Bergson, Abram, 141, 149
Blended payment, 15, 36, 89–90
Border prices, 49
Borrowing rate of interest, 52, 66
Bos, H.C., 107
Bowen, Howard, 43
Bridge cost and investment, 35, 40–41, 109–112, 119–122, 142–144, 152–153

Canada, 95, 106
Cash flow, 89–91
Caviar, individual demands, 26–27; as anoprosthetic, 29; versus road project; 148–149
Caviar demand, as anoprosthetic, 29
Central bank (discount) rate, 53
Chieftown, 155–157
Collection costs, 22, 37–38, 126
Community college, 41–42
Commuter train, 41–42
Congestion costs, 120–122
Congestion, theory of, 55–57
Consumer surplus, 7, 93, 98–99, 103–104, 139–147, 147–150
Consumption frontier, 66–72, 80–81
Continuously variable cost, 17–19
Cost-benefit analysis, 1–3, 63

Cost of living, 78, 82
Cost reduction criterion, 8, 130
CPI. *See* Cost of living
Crossover rate, 86–87
Crown corporations. *See* State-owned enterprises
Currie, J.M., 107
Customs duties. *See* Import duties

Dallas–Fort Worth area, 112
Depreciation, 16–20, 76, 89–91, 155–157
Discount rate, 7, 53, 64–71
Discounting or discount criterion, 6, 7
Discretely variable cost, 17–19
Discrimination in pricing, 23, 126–127
Dorfman, Robert, 10, 59
Double counting, 94–95
Dupuit, Jules, 11, 125, 127, 139–140, 149

Ecalpon, 26, 41, 57–58, 89, 106, 135, 154–155
Ecalpon Export Rail Line, 54
Ecalpon Hydro, 155–157
Eckstein, Otto, 10
Efficiency objective for public participation, 6, 21–26
Efficient-budget constraint, 3–4, 116–117
Elasticity of demand, 26–31
Equivalent traffic unit, 37, 38
ETU. *See* Equivalent traffic unit
Excise taxes, 48–49

Federal tax exemption, 53, 114
Feldstein, Martin, 59, 91
Ferry costs, 111, 118–119. *See also* Bridge cost and investment
Fiscal distortions, 48–52
Fisher, Irving, 91
Financial analysis, 75–77, 90
Financial Post, 7
Fixed capital, 156
Fixed cost, 16, 36
Foster, C.D., 59
Footbridge, 139–140
Fourth-power law, 18. *See also* AASHO coefficient
Free riders, 23
Fromm, Gary, 59

GDP, 96
General tax revenues, 110–112
Gittinger, J. Price, 10, 108
GNE. *See* Gross National Expenditure
GNP. *See* Gross National Product
Gross National Expenditure, 7, 96, 97
Gross National Product, 7, 49, 59, 95–97

Harberger, Arnold, 10, 59, 91, 141, 149
Harrison, A.J., 59
Haveman, Robert H., 59
Hicks, John, 146
Hirshleifer, Jack, 91
Historic cost, 155–156
Housing imputations, 106, 134–135

IBRD. *See* World Bank
Imaginary roots (for IRR), 88
Import duties, 49–52, 58–59, 135–137
Income distribution goals, 41–42, 131, 134, 144–147
Income distribution objective for public participation, 6, 21
Income transfers, 41–42, 57
Index number problems, 94, 100–102
Inflation, 9, 54–55, 151–154, 154–157
Infrastructure decisions, 8, 107–118, 118–128
Intensity of demand, 31. *See also* Inverse elasticity rule
Interest, 52–54. *See also* various individual interest categories
Interest as price component, 127
Internal rate of return, 67, 73–75, 78, 85–88
International Bank for Reconstruction and Development. *See* World Bank
Intertemporal production frontier, 7. *See also* Consumption frontier
Inverse elasticity rule, 31, 34
Investment expenditure, 16–20
IRR. *See* Internal rate of return
Isochronic cost, 17–20, 22, 41–42, 119, 125

Joint cost, 17–20, 125–127
Joint demand, 31–35

Koyck, L.M., 107

Labor and wage distortions, 46–48, 131–132, 133–137. *See also* Valuation of time
Labor-intensive projects, 130, 133
Lal, Deepak, 10, 108
Layard, Richard, 10, 59, 91
Legal–administrative efficiency, 22–23
Lending rate of interest, 66
Less-than-full-cost recovery, 6, 22–26, 68
Less-than-fully-employed economy. *See* Underdeveloped economy
Little, I.M.D., 10, 59
Lorie, James, 91
LTFCR. *See* Less-than-full-cost recovery
LTFE. *See* Underdeveloped economy

Maas, A., 10
MacArthur, J.D., 108
Mack, Ruth P., 59
Marginal degree of utility, 140, 146
Marginal productivity of capital, 52, 53, 68–73, 82, 107, 111
Marginal social cost, 56–57, 119–121
Marginal tax rate, 144
Marginal utility of money, 103, 145–147
Marglin, Stephen, 59, 91
Margolis, Julius, 59
Market distortions due to incorrect definition of costs, 47–48
Marshall, Alfred, 139, 145–147, 149
Marshallian consumer surplus, 145
McKean, R.N., 59
Mirrlees, James A., 10, 59
Mishan, E.J., 10
Moody's, 52, 72
MPK. *See* Marginal productivity of capital
MSC. *See* Marginal social cost
Multiple roots (for IRR), 88
Munby, Denys, 10
Murphy, J.A., 107
Musgrave, Richard, 21, 42
Meyers, Sumner, 59

National Academy of Sciences, 43
National income, 71–72, 94–96; as an

approach to benefit measurement, 93–98, 100–107; and index number problem, 100–102
National–political objectives for public participation, 21
Net National Income, 49
Net present value, 64–73, 77–78, 79–85, 87–88, 122–124
Network projects, 115–118
Newberry, D.M.G., 108
Nonexcludability, 23
Nonmarket benefits, 68–70, 109
NPV. *See* Net present value

Opportunity cost, 19, 156–157
Output-variable cost, 17–19, 36

Pearce, D.W., 10
Periodically recurring costs, 17–20
Petropon, 26
Physical criteria, 4, 7, 116–117
Police protection, as anoprosthetic demand, 23, 39, 40
Prest, Alan R., 9
Prime rate, 52, 82, 152
Profits criterion, 8, 89–91, 130
Public good, 21–23, 35, 43, 156. *See also* Anoprosthetic demand

Quarmby, D.A., 59

Real rate of interest, 52, 82
Recurring fixed cost, 17–20
Relative net present value, 84
Replacement cost, 54–55, 155–156
Revenue bonds, 53, 114, 152–153
"Rule of 72," 118, 125, 127

Sao Paulo, 97
Samuelson, Paul, 43
Savage, Leonard, 91
Schmitz, A., 107
Secularly underemployed economy. *See* Underdeveloped economy
Sen, Amartya, 59, 91
Shadow prices/values, 6, 45–59, 131, 134–137. *See also* individual types of distortion
Social indifference curve, 7; intertemporal, 68–72
Social rate of time preference, 52, 53

Socially efficient demand, 5, 116–117
SOE. *See* State-owned enterprises
Solomon, Ezra, 91
Soviet investment rules, 10
Special bond issues, 112–115
Stabilization objective for public participation, 6, 21
"Standard Methodology for Investment Allocation," 10
State-owned enterprises, 3, 4, 7, 42, 45, 64, 79, 83, 89, 98, 129, 152, 154
Staten Island. *See* Verrazano-Narrows Bridge
Statistics Canada, 59, 96
Steiner, Peter, 43
Strait of Georgia (British Columbia), 142
Sunk costs, 16, 156

Tax expenditures, 2
Third-structure taxes, 22. *See also* User charges
Time, value of. *See* Valuation of time
Time variable costs, 18–19, 37, 125
Tinbergen, J., 107
Traditional cost theory, 15
Traffic flows, 38
Transamazon highway, 116
True rate of interest, 52
Turvey, Ralph, 9

Underdeveloped economy, 8, 103–106, 129–138
Unemployment rate, 82
U.S. Bureau of Labor Statistics, 82
U.S. Department of Commerce, 59, 82
U.S. Joint Economic Committee, 10, 59
Urbams, 24–25
User charges, 68, 126, 132

Valuation of time, 48, 57
Variable inputs, 16–20
Venn diagram of users of cost-benefit analysis, 1–3
Verrazano-Narrows Bridge, 142, 150

Weisbrod, Burton, 59
Wall Street Journal, 7
World Bank, 10

About the Author

Alan Abouchar teaches economics at the University of Toronto. He has also taught at Yale University and the University of Maryland. Professor Abouchar is the author of four other books and numerous articles in leading professional journals and collections. He has served as a consultant to public sector agencies in North and South America, Europe, the Middle East, and Africa in the fields of industrial strategy, transportation policy, and regional economics. He holds graduate degrees in economics, statistics, and pure mathematics from the University of California, Berkeley (Ph.D., M.A.), New York University (A.M.), and York University (M.A.).

LIBRARY OF DAVIDSON COLLEGE

Books on regular loan may
...resented at th...